Field Guide to the Global Economy

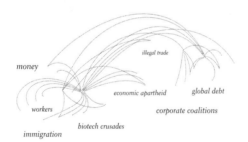

Field Guide to the Global Economy

SARAH ANDERSON AND
JOHN CAVANAGH WITH **THEA LEE**

and the **Institute for Policy Studies**

The New Press New York

© 2000 by Sarah Anderson, John Cavanagh, Thea Lee, and
the Institute for Policy Studies. All rights reserved.

Published in the United States by The New Press, New York
Distributed by W. W. Norton & Company, Inc., New York

Library of Congress Cataloging-in-Publication Data

Anderson, Sarah (Sarah Denny)
field guide to the global economy / Sarah Anderson and John Cavanagh
with Thea Lee; and the Institute for Policy Studies.
    p.   cm.
Includes bibliographical references.
1. International trade Handbooks, manuals, etc. 2. Investments,
Foreign handbooks, manuals, etc. 3. International finance Handbooks,
manuals, etc. 4. International business enterprises Handbooks,
manuals, etc. 5. Social responsibility of business Handbooks, manuals, etc.
6. International economic relations Handbooks, manuals, etc.
I. Cavanagh, John. II. Lee, Thea. III. Institute for Policy Studies.
IV. Title.
HF1379.A697 1999
658.8´48—dc21 99-15595
        CIP

The New Press was established in 1990 as a not-for-profit alternative
to the large, commercial publishing houses currently dominating
the book publishing industry. The New Press operates in the public
interest rather than for private gain, and is committed to publishing,
in innovative ways, works of educational, cultural, and community
value that are often deemed insufficiently profitable.

www.thenewpress.com

Printed in the United States of America

Contents

FOREWORD
Barbara Ehrenreich

Watch the commercials on prime time CNN and you'll see enticing images of globalization. Slender yuppies of both sexes stride from airplanes into conference rooms in London or Zurich. Executives in company headquarters confer by computer with engineers in Frankfurt or bankers in Hong Kong, agonizing over how best to preserve the rain forests or develop a life-saving new drug. Cell phones dialed in muddy backwaters of the Southern Hemisphere ring in elegant corner offices. Investments zip through modems at the speed of light. On our television screens, the tantalizing visual clichés flash by one after another—the Eiffel Tower, the Taj Mahal, palm-lined beaches, locals dancing in native costume. We are all connected now, is the message, in one big vibrant, pulsing, global adventure.

There are other, not so pretty, images of globalization that seldom appear on television. While the corporate managers fly business class from one financial capital to another, laborers risk their lives sneaking across borders in search of a few dollars more a day in pay. While executives plot corporate strategy over room-service meals, teen-aged girls stitch garments and assemble toys for twelve-hour shifts in airless sweatshops. In this, far less glamorous, stratum of the global economy, Brazilian and Philippine villages are destroyed by logging companies, while towns in Michigan and Ohio are wiped out by downsizing and plant relocations. You won't find many commercials set around the maquiladoras of northern Mexico or the ramshackle factories of Mumbai, India, where globalization means anxiety, long hours of hard work, and shantytowns with open sewers.

The *Field Guide to the Global Economy* connects the dots between these two worlds of globalization. The problem, according to the authors, is not so much that the world is so tightly linked now—by trade, investments, and high-speed telecommunications—but that the links converge in such a small number of hands. There are 193 nations in the world, many of them ostensibly democratic, but most of them are dwarfed by the corporations that alone decide what will be produced, and where, and how much people will be paid to do the work. In effect, these multinational enterprises have become a kind of covert world government—motivated solely by profit and unaccountable to any citizenry. Only a small group of humans on the planet, roughly overlapping the world's 475-member billionaire's club, rule the global economy. And wherever globalization impinges, inequality deepens. From Mexico to Japan, the rich are getting richer while the poor are becoming more desperate and numerous.

The solution does not lie in a retreat to nationalism and rigid protectionism, or in hermetically sealed economies like that of North Korea. Potentially, globalization could lead to a safer, more peaceful and—who knows?—more interesting world, if, for example, international trade agreements were designed to promote human rights and preserve cultural diversity, instead of just to ease the accumulation of wealth by those who already have more than they know what to do with. But that would be a very different kind of globalization, one in which people who are not "players"—investors or executives—also have a voice.

There's only one way to get there, and it's through even more connectedness, this time among the millions of people at the grubby end of the global economy: labor unions in Mexico linking up with religious groups in Europe; students in California protesting on behalf of workers in Vietnam; women's groups in Massachusetts exchanging information about pharmaceuticals with their counterparts in India or Peru. What you get, as the grassroots networks expand and link up across national boundaries, is something far more exciting than the dash for profits glorified on CNN commercials. It's called solidarity, which is an old-fashioned word for the love between people who may never meet each other, but share a vision of justice and democracy and are willing to support each other in the struggle to achieve it. This is our adventure for the new millennium—recapturing the global economy from its corporate high-jackers. Don't be left out.

Paris
London
Dublin
Berlin
Madrid
Valencia
Barcelona
Rome
Naples
Athens
Tunis
Algiers
Gibraltar
Rabat
Lisbon
Porto
Tripoli
Alexandria
Cairo
Istanbul
Ankara
Izmir
Adana
Amman
Baghdad
Al Basrah
Tehran
Shiraz
Baku
Ashkhabad
Kabul
Tashkent
Frunze
Alma Ata
Islamabad
Lahore
New Delhi
Jaipur
Agra
Kanpur
Calcutta
Varanasi
Karachi
Muscat
Bombay
Indore
Bangalore
Coimbatore
Colombo
Riyadh
SAUDI ARABIA
YEMEN
Sanaa
Kiev
Moscow
Kharkov
Volgograd
Donetsk
Krasnodar
Saratov
Chisinau
Krakow
Warsaw
Minsk
ALGERIA
LIBYA
EGYPT
SUDAN
Khartoum
Asmara
ETHIOPIA
Addis Abbaba
Mogadishu
NIGER
CHAD
NDjamena
MALI
MAURITANIA
Nouakchott
Niamey
Bamako
Abuja
Lagos
Lome
Monrovia
Yaounde
Bangui
Mbandaka
CENTRAL AFRICAN REPUBLIC
CONGO
ZAIRE
Libreville
Brazzaville
Kinshasa
Luanda
Matadi
ANGOLA
Huambo
Windhoek
Walvis Bay
Nairobi
KENYA
Dar es Salaam
TANZANIA
Lubumbashi
Lilongwe
Lusaka
Harare
Bulawayo
ZAMBIA
Gaborone
Pretoria
Johannesburg
Maputo
Durban
SOUTH AFRICA
Antananarivo
Indian Ocean
Ocean
Canary Islands
WESTERN SAHARA
Ponta Delgada
Praia

RUSSIA
Krasnoyarsk
Novosibirsk
Irkutsk
Ulaanbaatar
Omsk
Karaganda
MONGOLIA
Qiqihar
Harbin
Jilin
Vladivostok
Changchung
Fuxin
Fushun
Pyongyang
Sapporo
Sendai
Tokyo
JAPAN
Osaka
Seoul
Kita-kyushu
Beijing
Tianjin
Baotou
Taiyuan
Kaifeng
Qingdao
Yinchuan
Xining
Lanzhou
Xian
Hefei
Shanghai
Ningbo
Wenzhou
Wuhan
Mianyang
Chengdu
Yueyang
Fuzhou
Taipei
TAIWAN
Chongqing
Guiyang
Shantou
Hong Kong
Kunming
Dukou
Urumqi
Frunze
Alma Ata
KYRGYZSTAN
Tashkent
TAJIKISTAN
Ashkhabad
Tehran
Baghdad
Al Basrah
Shiraz
Kabul
AFGHANISTAN
Islamabad
CHINA
Lahore
New Delhi
NEPAL
Agra
Kathmandu
BHUTAN
PAKISTAN
Karachi
Jaipur
Kanpur
Chittagong
Hanoi
Muscat
Indore
Calcutta
MYANMAR
LAOS
Vientiane
Nagpur
Varanasi
Bay of Bengal
THAILAND
VIETNAM
Bombay
Hyderabad
Rangoon
Bangkok
KAMPUCHEA
Saigon
INDIA
Bangalore
Madras
Phnom Penh
Coimbatore
SRI LANKA
Colombo
South China Sea
Manila
PHILIPPINES
Davao
Kuala Lumpur
MALAYSIA
Medan
Singapore
Palembang
Jakarta
Makasar
INDONESIA
Surabaya
Bandung
Indian Ocean
Pacific Ocean
PAPUA NEW GUINEA
Port Moresby
Darwin
Timor Sea
AUSTRALIA
Adelaide
Brisbane
Sydney
Perth

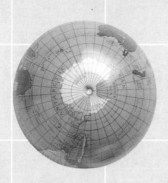
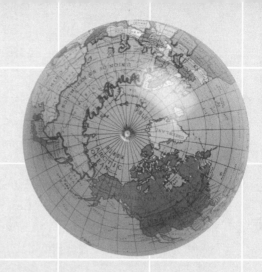

INTRODUCTION
Corporate Globalization

Most of what we eat, drink, wear, drive, smoke, and watch is the product of firms that are now global in their operations. Once wedded to local communities, many of these firms now operate in dozens of countries on all continents save Antarctica. Increasing numbers are owned by shareholders in many different countries. The revenues of these privately-owned giants rival the gross national product of many countries.

For those consumers who can afford their wares, these firms offer a dazzling array of goods and services around the world. They are also moving trillions of dollars across borders at lightning speed. Their power over our lives, our planet, and our democratic institutions has never been greater.

Indeed, most governments around the world now seek to assist corporate-led globalization and pursue policies that enhance the ability of corporations to move their products, money, and factories around the globe more quickly and with less impediment from regulations. New and proposed regional and global trade and investment deals aim to lift further the remaining barriers to trade and investment flows across borders.

Yet a powerful backlash has been gaining strength in dozens of countries. Debates rage around the world as to whether such corporate-driven globalization helps or hinders the aspirations of the majority of people on earth. The debates are erupting across college campuses, in labor unions, church basements, parliaments, city halls, and at millions of dinner tables around the world. This is a healthy development because for decades government policy around the global economy was shaped by a few people, many from the corporate sector, who were quite insulated from the public.

In these debates, those promoting an acceleration of globalization point to the benefits to consumers and workers who find jobs in global factories. Those who make up what is often referred to as a growing "backlash against globalization" point to adverse impacts on equality, natural resources, work, food, communities, culture, and even democracy. And, since the emergence of what we call the "global financial casino" in the late 1990s, millions of people are increasingly anxious about financial crises in one region spreading like wildfire to other countries with devastating economic and environmental consequences.

In the United States, polls show that those opposed to current "pro-globalization" policies outnumber those in favor. In 1997, for the first time in modern U.S. history, citizen groups successfully pressed the U.S. Congress to reject a bill authorizing the President free rein in pursuing trade deals. Likewise in many developing countries, trade and investment liberalization has sparked passionate protests, from riots in Indonesia to a guerrilla uprising in southern Mexico.

This book is structured to help nurture both the debates around the global economy and the actions that people take to get involved. It does this by:

- ◑ **sketching out the history and status of global flows of goods and services, money, and people**
- ◑ **explaining what is new about globalization today**
- ◑ **addressing ten common claims of globalization backers**
- ◑ **describing the major institutions and policies driving globalization**
- ◑ **highlighting people's efforts to stop, slow down, or change the course of globalization.**

At the very least, we hope that this book helps you in discussions with friends, colleagues, and family members. If you are moved to act, we end the book with a guide to some of the more dynamic groups around the world that are grappling with the global economy. All of them need your help.

3

money

biotech cr

workers

immigration

1. What *Is* Economic Globalization?

Economic globalization consists of the flows of goods and services, capital, and people across national borders. Although globalization has occurred for centuries in each of these realms, it is going through a period of rapid change. Understanding the dynamics of today's global economy requires some knowledge of what came before.

illegal trade

global debt

corporate coalitions

des   *economic apartheid*

History

PRE-1492

Prior to the time of Columbus, most economic activity in the world was highly localized. People ate, drank, worked, and used products that in large part came from close to home. Goods or people from other lands were rare and came from one of three sources:

1. ARMIES: From Alexander the Great to Attila the Hun to the Crusades, armies covered vast distances in pursuit of conquest. Many returned home with plundered goods and slaves from the conquered lands.

2. TRAVELERS AND EXPLORERS: From the Vikings to Marco Polo, people traveled great distances to reach new worlds, often bringing home exotic foods, spices, crafts, and other riches. Indeed, during the early fifteenth century, a Ming Dynasty Chinese emperor built a vast fleet that sailed as far as East Africa, returning with zebras, giraffes, and other live animals.[1]

3. TRADERS: For hundreds of years Chinese and Arab traders plied routes across Asia, the Middle East, and Northern Africa.

Despite these early forays over the millennia, the expense, danger, and uncertainty of long trips limited exchanges, and most people remained untouched by events in other lands. All of this was to change with the onset of what our history books have called the Age of Exploration.

1492–1945 Empire and the Colonial Division of Labor[2]

Columbus did more than sail into the Western Hemisphere in a mistaken quest for an eastern route to the riches of "the Indies." By introducing sugar, oranges, and other products into the hemisphere and by beginning the large-scale extraction of its gold and other minerals, he and other "explorers" began the transformation of who does what in which part of the world. Their behavior toward natives was vicious, treating the Indians "not as beasts, for beasts are treated properly at times, but like the excrement in a public square," according to Friar Bartolomé de las Casas, who accompanied Columbus on his first voyage and later became bishop of Chiapas, Mexico.

Beginning in the late fifteenth century, European powers financed explorations to what would become known as Africa, Asia, and the Western Hemisphere. Within decades, explorations turned to conquest and colonial authorities directed movements of goods, capital, and people into a new colonial division of labor, some of which persists today. During these four and a half centuries, Spain, Portugal, England, France, the Netherlands, Belgium, Germany, Italy, and later the United States and Japan rearranged economic activity in much of Asia, Africa, and Latin America in the following ways:

MANUFACTURING IN THE RICH COUNTRIES: Colonial authorities sought to undermine indigenous textile manufacturing in the colonies in order to create new markets for the textiles, clothing, and machinery of the colonial powers. Persia, India, the Philippines, and other lands had quite advanced textile centers that were undercut by colonial trade. Cheaper manufactured products from Europe flooded into the colonies which, in turn, were pressed to shift more and more land and people to the production of minerals and agricultural products for export. Only in the United States did the textile industry thrive after colonization.

MINERALS: Columbus sailed west to find gold for Spain. Despite the enslavement and relatively quick annihilation of local populations, little was found in the Caribbean. Much more was soon found in the Aztec and Incan empires of this "new world" and millions of indigenous people died in the mines or from disease spread by the Europeans. As industry flourished in Europe so too did the demand for copper, tin, bauxite, and other minerals from Latin America and Africa.

AGRICULTURE: To meet the requirements of England's textile mills for cotton and other natural fibers, and the European demand for the luxuries of sugar, coffee, cocoa, tea, and bananas, plantations growing these commodities were carved from forests around the world. Sugar was the greatest early destroyer, beginning with the Portuguese leveling of Brazilian forests in the 1530s and followed by other colonizers across the Caribbean. Hence began the destruction of the world's great tropical rain forests. Colonial trading companies directed much of this traffic until the nineteenth century when the private Japanese, European, and U.S. firms that are the forbears of some of today's largest global corporations and banks were incorporated.

PEOPLE: Flourishing colonial economic activity in the Caribbean, Brazil, and the southern United States soon exterminated so much of the indigenous population that new labor supplies were needed. Colonial authorities vastly expanded the African slave trade by linking West Africa with the Western Hemisphere. Up to thirteen million Africans were shipped across the Atlantic Ocean between 1444 and 1870, at least two million of them dying in transit of murder, disease, suicide, or malnutrition. While many cut sugar, others sweated in the tobacco, cotton, and rice fields of North America or in the gold and diamond mines of Brazil.

The transformation of most colonies into exporters of one or two minerals or agricultural products twisted those economies into dependence on products over whose price and marketing they had no control.

Since World War II: New Divisions

When World War II broke out across Europe and Asia, the world economy reflected a rather uniform division of labor. In the richer countries of Europe and in the United States, Canada, Japan, and Australia, large corporations sourced the bulk of the world's minerals and agricultural commodities from countries and colonies of Latin America, Africa, and Asia. Today, this basic division has changed radically.

While the richer countries of Europe and North America along with Japan, Australia, and New Zealand still largely export industrial products, among the poorer nations, six groups of countries have emerged:

1. BIG EMERGING MARKETS (in black below). These countries have entered the industrial age to become large-scale manufacturers of a broad range of products. However, they are still poor by many measures, and the global financial crisis of the late 1990s posed a serious setback to the incomes and aspirations of several of these countries.[3]

2. WOULD-BE BEMs (in gray, italics below). These have moved beyond simple assembly of clothing and electronics into a few more diversified and industrial and service sectors.[4]

The Big Emerging Markets (BEMs) and the Would-Be BEMs

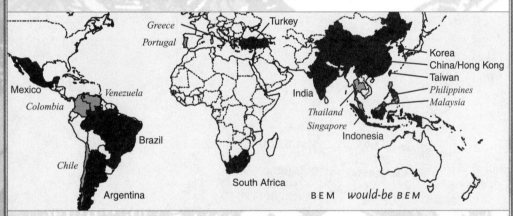

3. OPEC NATIONS. These oil-exporting countries have been able to import whole factories for their suddenly affluent populations, but by and large they lack the scientific and engineering expertise to develop their own industrial bases: Venezuela and Indonesia are also OPEC members, but we have listed them in would-be BEMs and BEMs, respectively.

4. FORMER COMMUNIST ECONOMIES. Despite a relatively high state of industrialization, most of the 26 former Soviet bloc nations are finding it difficult to compete for foreign investment with the industrializing enclaves of Asia and Latin America. The rapid shift from socialism to deregulated market economies reliant on external finance left many of these countries vulnerable to the fickleness of the global financial casino. In some cases economic crisis has exacerbated longstanding ethnic tensions.

5. RAW MATERIAL EXPORTERS AND LIGHT MANUFACTURERS.
About 40 countries have little heavy industry beyond assembly, packing, and processing facilities and are suppliers of simple manufactured goods or raw materials for export. Some also earn income from tourism.

6. LEAST DEVELOPED COUNTRIES. About 60 countries, mostly all in Africa, are so poor that their economic connection with the rest of the world is pretty much limited to minimal trade and investment and dwindling foreign aid.

Colonial Division of Labor still Persists for Many Countries
Among groups five and six on the preceding pages, there are thirty-five countries in Latin America, Africa, and Asia that still gain two fifths or more of export earnings from one or two agricultural or mineral products:

Latin America
Belize (sugar)
Chile (copper and metal ores)
Costa Rica (coffee and fruit)
Cuba (sugar)
Dominica (iron and fruit)
Guadeloupe (sugar and fruit)
Guyana (gold and sugar)
Honduras (fruit and coffee)
Jamaica (minerals)
Panama (fruit)
Paraguay (vegetable oil and cotton)
Saint Lucia (fruit)

Africa

Burkina Faso (cotton)
Burundi (coffee)
Ivory Coast (cocoa and coffee)
Ethiopia (coffee)
Ghana (cocoa and precious stones)
Kenya (tea and coffee)
Madagascar (coffee and spices)
Malawi (tobacco)
Mauritania (iron ore)
Mozambique (fish and fruit)
Reunion (sugar)

Rwanda (coffee)
Senegal (fish and vegetable oil)
Seychelles (fish)
Sierra Leone (precious stones)
Sudan (cotton and vegetables)
Uganda (coffee)

Asia

Burma (wood and vegetables)
Fiji (sugar)
Maldives (fish)
Papua New Guinea (gold and metal ores)
Solomon Islands (wood)
Tonga (vegetables)

Global Flows Today

This history leaves a world where peoples and countries are increasingly intertwined. Here is a current snapshot of the state of the three main cross-border flows: goods and services, finance, and people.

A. TRADE IN GOODS AND SERVICES

Through numerous rounds of negotiations or pressure from multilateral agencies, most countries in the world have substantially lifted barriers to trade in goods and services over the last two decades. This "liberalization," combined with new technologies, has made trade increasingly important to the world economy.

Main Goods Traded Across Borders
(see pie chart on following page)

- cars, trucks, and car parts
- petroleum products to run the cars and other machinery
- textiles, footwear, and clothing

Together these three items account for almost one out of every four goods traded.[5] The other three quarters consists of millions of other products, led by machinery, electronic goods, aircraft, pharmaceuticals, and paper.

World exports of goods and services as a percentage of world output[6]

1870	1913	1973	1996
5.0	8.7	12.1	23.6

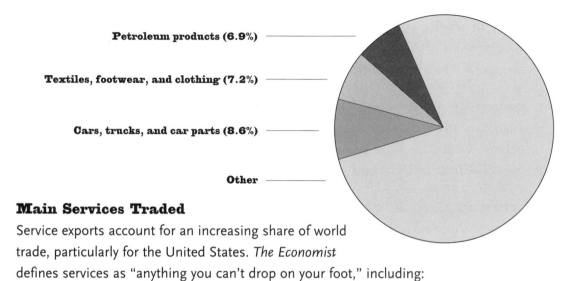

Petroleum products (6.9%)

Textiles, footwear, and clothing (7.2%)

Cars, trucks, and car parts (8.6%)

Other

Main Services Traded

Service exports account for an increasing share of world trade, particularly for the United States. *The Economist* defines services as "anything you can't drop on your foot," including:

- tourism and travel
- communications, computer, and information services
- advertising
- legal services
- all forms of entertainment

The United States enjoys one of its biggest trade surpluses in the products of Hollywood, even though most of the entertainment companies are headquartered in Japan, Britain, Germany, and other countries.

Service Exports as a percentage of Total Exports[7]

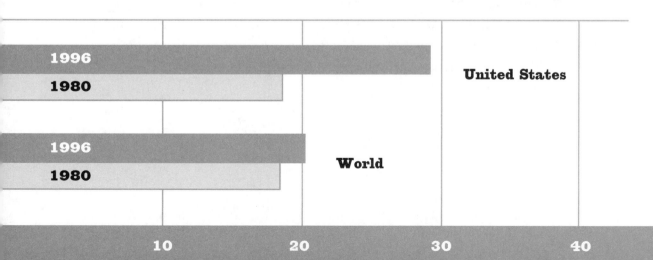

1996
1980

United States

1996
1980

World

10   20   30   40

Illegal Trade

A rising share of global trade does not appear in official trade figures because it is illegal. The biggest components of illegal trade include:

DRUGS The globalization of trade, finance, and communications has made it easier to transport illicit drugs and launder the proceeds. The United Nations estimates the value of the drug trade to be about $400 billion a year, or 8 percent of all international trade.[8]

WEAPONS No reliable statistics exist for the trafficking of weapons. However, a report by the Federation of American Scientists claims that the trade in "light" weapons (assault rifles, mortars, grenades, and land mines) is flourishing as governments downsize their militaries in the wake of the Cold War and seek cash customers for their arsenals.[9]

PEOPLE The United Nations estimates that four million people per year fall prey to trafficking networks, resulting in profits to criminal groups of up to $7 billion.[10] These figures include both international trade as well as "internal" trafficking (e.g., when women are forced to migrate from rural areas to work in urban sex industries). However, cross-border trade is clearly on the rise, particularly as increasing numbers of women flee rampant unemployment in former Soviet-bloc nations and migrate to the United States, Western Europe, Japan, and elsewhere.

ENDANGERED ANIMALS Interpol estimates that illegal trade in wildlife involves at least $5 billion annually.[11] Animals killed or caught alive by poachers wind up as handbags, circus acts, medicines, pets, and jewelry for customers all around the world. A World Wildlife Fund investigation of more than 100 traditional medicine stores in the United States and Canada revealed that 50 percent offered illegal substances derived from endangered species such as tigers, rhinoceros, and leopards.[12]

Much of Trade Not "Free"

Although governments across the globe have lifted numerous barriers to international trade, significant protections remain and new ones are added every day. In theory, these mechanisms can promote positive social goals, such as protections for the environment, public health, or stable jobs. However, in the current reality, they are often designed to promote the interests of the politically powerful. Government interventions in trade can take the form of:

1. BARRIERS TO IMPORTS: Countries use a range of mechanisms to control the flow of imports, including tariffs (taxes on the value of goods for import) and so-called "nontariff barriers," such as outright bans on certain products or quotas to limit the amount of products imported.

Peanut Pork: Import restrictions make peanuts one of the most heavily protected U.S. agricultural commodities. However, these protections do little to help average U.S. farmers because only a select group of producers have the right to sell peanuts for U.S. consumption, for which they receive prices that are double the world market price. Why has this group received such privileged treatment? Many say the policy has survived in the free-trade climate thanks to the efforts of Sen. Jesse Helms, the powerful chair of the Foreign Relations Committee, and an ally of peanut producers in his state of North Carolina.

2. EXPORT PROMOTION: Most governments provide financial support to companies involved in exports or foreign investment. In the United States, the Export-Import Bank provides loans and loan guarantees to exporting firms, while the Overseas Private Investment Corporation provides insurance to U.S. companies investing overseas. Worldwide, such agencies support exports totaling $432.2 billion, about 10.4 percent of total world exports.[13] In addition, governments also commonly fund programs to market products abroad and sometimes subsidize export industries.

Military: What President Eisenhower called the "military industrial complex" continues to have many friends in Washington. In 1995, the U.S. government spent $6.9 billion promoting the weapons exports of large U.S. firms, twelve times as much as it spent promoting exports in environmental technologies, according to the National Commission for Economic Conversion and Disarmament.[14]

B. INTERNATIONAL FINANCIAL FLOWS

For most of history, finance followed and facilitated the production and trade of goods and services. In the late nineteenth and early twentieth centuries, large privately owned banks emerged in North America, Europe, and Japan. They developed close relationships with large manufacturing firms and financed their activities around the world. Once established in other countries, they expanded their financing to firms from other nations.

In addition to banks, today individuals, corporations, and other institutions (e.g., pension funds) are extensively involved in cross-border financial transactions. Since 1980, all international financial flows have accelerated rapidly, at a pace far outstripping trade flows. Governments have facilitated this boom by "liberalizing" (lifting barriers to) investment. Liberalizing in this sense might include removing a requirement that large loans get government approval or improving the speed with which funds may be transferred into and out of the country. According to the United Nations, more than 100 countries have passed such laws during the past fifteen years.

Financial Flows Outpace Trade Flows

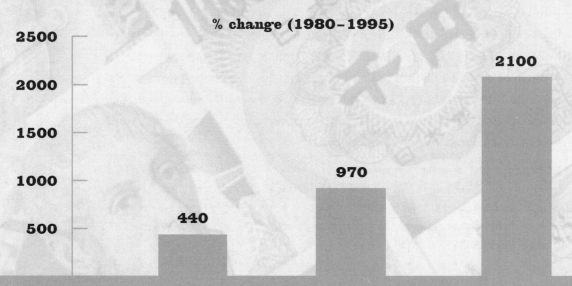

% change (1980–1995)

2500
2000
1500
1000
500

440 — Value of World Merchandise Trade
970 — Value of World Stock Exchanges
2100 — Value of Foreign Exchange Transactions

International financial flows include public and private lending:
Public lending comes from governments or from government-funded international financial institutions (e.g., a World Bank loan to the government of Honduras for road construction). This is sometimes called "official" lending. The main sources are the World Bank, the International Monetary Fund, regional development banks, and government aid agencies.

Private financial flows fall into three main categories:
1. FOREIGN DIRECT INVESTMENT (FDI) involves a corporation purchasing a lasting interest in, and degree of influence over, the management of a business in another country (e.g., General Motors and Ford purchasing plants in Mexico).
2. PORTFOLIO INVESTMENT is the cross-border purchase of stocks, bonds, derivatives, and other financial assets. It differs from direct investment in that the investor is generally not seeking management control of local companies (e.g., a U.S. citizen's purchase of a few shares of stock in a German-owned company).
3. DEBT FLOWS include commercial bank loans and bonds (e.g., a Citicorp loan to a Brazilian firm to purchase new equipment).

Financial Flows and the Developing World

ECONOMIC APARTHEID

Although public lending has declined somewhat during the 1990s, private financial flows have boomed, particularly into the developing world. Developing countries' share of total foreign investment jumped from 20 percent of the total in 1990 to 34 percent in 1995–96.[15] However, this boom has been concentrated in China and a handful of other "new emerging markets." Hence, the prospect of global economic apartheid has emerged wherein the rich countries grow slowly, a small group of developing nations grows rapidly (and are wracked with volatility), and the bulk of poorer nations grow slowly or not at all.

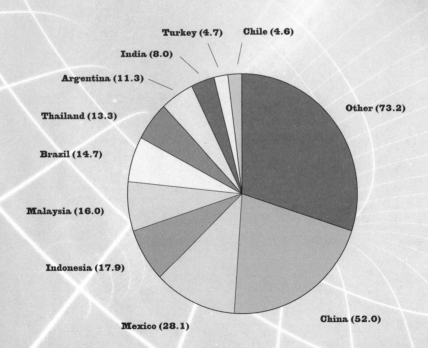

Three fourths of private financial flows into the developing world is going to ten countries[16] (1996 = $ billions)

Turkey (4.7) Chile (4.6)
India (8.0)
Argentina (11.3)
Other (73.2)
Thailand (13.3)
Brazil (14.7)
Malaysia (16.0)
Indonesia (17.9)
China (52.0)
Mexico (28.1)

Crisis in the Global Financial Casino

Some have argued that this capital influx is the developing world's ticket to prosperity. Others claim that the flood of capital, particularly the short-term portfolio flows, has made countries vulnerable to economic instability while doing little to improve the lives of ordinary people.

Financial Flows to Developing Countries ($ billions)[17]

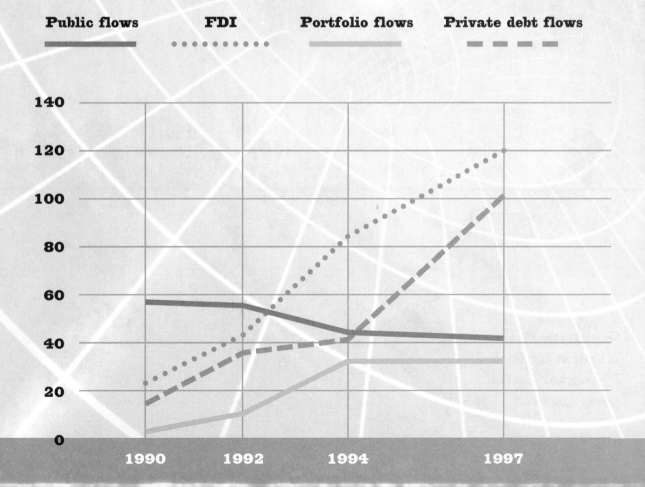

Public flows · · · · · · · FDI · · · · · · · · · Portfolio flows · · · · · Private debt flows

The Chain Reaction of Global Financial Crises

In a world of financial deregulation, a crisis in one country can spread like wild-fire across borders and even oceans. Consider the Asian financial crisis that began in mid-1997, when nervous Western investors began pulling billions of dollars worth of short-term "hot money" out of Asian countries whose economies were strapped by huge external debts. This began a chain reaction of currency devaluations and stock market plunges throughout Asia and into other regions of the world. By the end of 1998, numerous countries showed negative economic growth while their citizens struggled with rampant unemployment, bankruptcies and in some cases political unrest. Two years into the crisis, an estimated 27 million workers had lost jobs in the five worst-hit Asian countries alone (Philippines, Indonesia, Malaysia, Thailand, and Korea).[18]

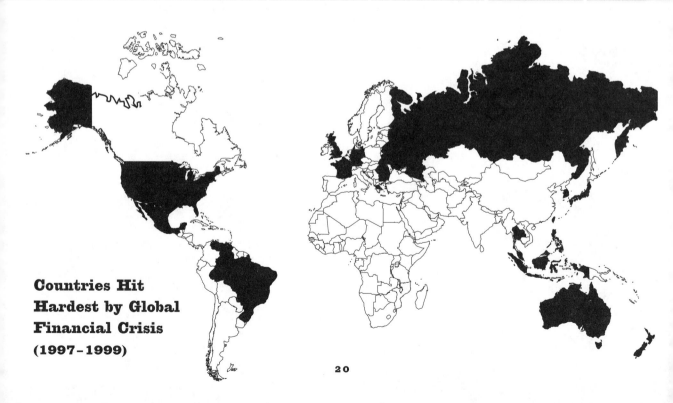

Countries Hit Hardest by Global Financial Crisis (1997–1999)

Debt Crisis Persists

Large sums of the financial flows to the developing world in recent decades have been loans. Hence, poor countries owe ever greater sums of money to banks in rich nations and to international financial institutions like the World Bank and the International Monetary Fund. The total debt burden for all developing countries is more than $2 trillion.[19]

© 1998 magill, jr.

How debt affects:

POOR COUNTRIES

To keep up with payments on their debt, poor countries often divert resources from meeting their people's basic needs. According to the international coalition Jubilee 2000:

- Mozambique spent twice as much in 1996 on debt payments as it spent on health and education, while 25 percent of that country's children died of infectious diseases.
- Nicaragua's debt repayments exceeded total spending on social programs, while 75 percent of the population lived below the poverty line.
- Uganda spent $17 on debt repayments for every $3 spent on health care; yet 25 percent of children died from preventable disease.

THE UNITED STATES

Meanwhile, the United States and other richer nations are also affected by what has been called The Debt Boomerang:[20]

1. Global Warming: Indebted countries are more likely to plunder their forests for export revenue or to clear forest lands for plantation crops destined for other lands.
2. Job Loss: Debtor countries are less able to purchase U.S. products, resulting in job loss in U.S. export industries.
3. Immigration: Dire economic consequences at home drive millions of people to seek a living in the United States and other rich countries.

Signs of Chaos	Description

CURRENCY DEVALUATION

When a government increases the amount of its currency it will exchange with other currencies at current exchange rates. For example, three weeks after Brazil devalued in January 1999, the amount of its currency (the real) needed to purchase $1 had jumped from 1.25 to more than 2. Most governments try to avoid sharp devaluations by hiking interest rates and using foreign reserves to buy up the local currency. However, big-time speculators can undermine these efforts by selling off vast amounts of a currency considered to be shaky.

PLUNGING STOCK MARKET

Fearing that the decade-long flood of investment into Asia had created a bubble that was about to burst, investors began selling off stocks with values thought to be inflated. Markets in the United States and elsewhere outside Asia also experienced record one-day plunges. Some analysts said the U.S. market's volatility was partly due to worries that U.S. firms would be hurt by an import surge from desperate Asian nations.

NEGATIVE ECONOMIC GROWTH

The standard measure of growth is the rate of increase in the Gross Domestic Product (GDP), which is the value of goods and services produced by an economy. In 1996, the Asian region had the world's highest GDP growth rates, averaging about 8 percent. But in 1998, many of these former stars fell into the negative. The most dramatic drop was in Indonesia, which had 8 percent GDP growth in 1996 and a 15 percent drop in 1998.

Impact

Nations Affected 1997-99

Over time, the devaluation should make the country's exports more competitive, but only if markets for the products exist. Yet, because it takes more of the local currency to buy foreign goods and make payments on foreign debt, prices rise and government budgets are strained. Also, debtors suffer from interest rates kept high to prevent further devaluation.

Thailand, Malaysia, Indonesia, Philippines, Brazil, Russia, Korea

U.S.: Exports to the devaluation countries dropped and imports from them increased, threatening some U.S. jobs.

Stock market plunges quickly erode domestic and foreign investor confidence, often leading to greater capital outflows.

Thailand, Malaysia, Singapore, Philippines, England, United States, Japan, Australia, Mexico, Korea, Taiwan, Indonesia, France, Germany

U.S.: Market plunged after bad news from Russia and Brazil, but bounced back rapidly. Continued instability could lead to consumer anxiety and lower spending.

Crisis nations import less, causing a decline in world commodities prices. For example, from June 1997 to August 1998, prices for oil dropped 30 percent, coffee 43 percent, and gold 17 percent.[21]

Japan, Indonesia, Korea, Malaysia, Philippines, Thailand, Hong Kong, Singapore, Russia, New Zealand, Venezuela, Bulgaria, Romania, Ukraine

U.S.: Countries suffering from depressed prices purchased fewer U.S. goods.

C. FLOWS OF PEOPLE

Global flows of people have been nearly as dynamic as flows of goods and capital. International migrants (people who have moved from one country to another) number about 100 million, or about 2 percent of the world's population.[22] People flows are also connected to capital flows. Workers follow economic opportunities. Often, they also send economic resources back to their homeland. Immigrants living in the United States sent home an estimated $20.7 billion in 1996, up from $9.2 billion in 1985.[23] Worldwide, such remittances are estimated to be about $67 billion.[24]

Liberalization Hasn't Extended to People

Although governments have facilitated the free flow of goods and capital, the trend has been to increase restrictions on the movement of people across borders. Virtually all the wealthier nations in the world have enacted legislation in the past several years to place stricter limits on immigration flows. Europe is the notable exception, although their liberalization of people flows applies mainly to people from European Union countries. Thus, although emigration continues to serve as somewhat of a safety valve for countries in economic crisis, the current trend is to reduce these opportunities.

In the United States

At a time when immigrants make up a much smaller percentage of the population than they did early in the century, Congress passed a law in 1996 to stem future flows by erecting new barriers to legal and illegal immigration and increasing financial obligations on sponsors of immigrants.

Percentage of U.S. Population that is foreign-born

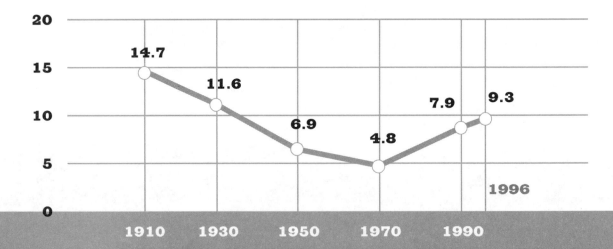

Execs the Exception

The United States, along with Canada and Mexico, did ease restrictions on cross-border movements through the North American Free Trade Agreement (NAFTA)—but only for business executives and professionals. Likewise in Europe and Asia, a number of countries have passed laws to make migration easier for highly skilled workers or those with money, but harder for the unskilled and the poor. Worldwide, an estimated 25 million people work outside their home country for global companies, moving across borders with few impediments.[25] In Canada, even criminals appear to be welcome, as long as they have enough cash. An ad in *Latin Trade* magazine promises "guaranteed immigration to Canada, even with a criminal record" with the purchase of a Fleet Rent-a-Car franchise.

II. What's *New* About the Global Economy?

Many people ask whether economic globalization is really that new or different. Although globalization has been around for several centuries, at least seven aspects of it are new.

A. HI-TECH GLOBAL ASSEMBLY LINE

Because of trade and investment liberalization (combined with improved communication and transportation technology), companies today can set up plants or subsidiaries wherever the costs are lowest. The expense of coordinating such far-flung operations is commonly outweighed by savings in wages, taxes, and the cost of conforming to environmental and other regulations. Richard Longworth's *Global Squeeze*[1] describes a Caterpillar plant in Toronto that takes in parts from other Caterpillar factories around the world—winches from Brazil, engines from Japan, axles from Belgium, transmissions from the United States. The plant then assembles these parts and exports the final product to countries around the world—including the ones where the parts came from in the first place.

A global assembly line for certain products is not new. As long ago as the 1970s, certain "labor-intensive" processes such as sewing apparel and assembling electronic goods were farmed out to factories in Asia, the Caribbean, and on the U.S.–Mexico border. A workforce made up largely of women workers, denied basic rights, assembled imported inputs for export abroad. What is new is that a number of poorer countries, led by China and Mexico, now have the infrastructure to house practically any industrial or service operation—including production of high-tech, capital-intensive products such as automobiles and aircraft. For example, Ford, Boeing, and other global corporations are now setting up state-of-the-art manufacturing plants in countries where wages and other costs are kept extremely low through repression.

Trading Inside the Corporate Family

One result of the international division of production is that roughly a third of world trade is not between countries but between one part of a global firm and an affiliate of that same firm. For example, when General Electric ships parts of machinery to its own subsidiary in Nuevo Laredo, Mexico, it is essentially "trading with itself." From 1982 to 1994, such "intra-firm" trade increased significantly as a share of U.S.–parent company trade. Exports shipped to their foreign affiliates rose from 31 to 42 percent, while imports sourced from their foreign affiliates rose from 36 to 50 percent. Intra-firm trade dominates exchange across the U.S.–Mexico border.

TAX LOOPHOLE

Intra-firm trade offers corporations the opportunity to avoid taxes by setting prices in order to maximize losses for subsidiaries in countries with high tax rates and maximize profits in tax havens. This type of accounting chicanery is known as transfer pricing.

OPPOSITE OF FREE TRADE

It is often argued that one of the benefits from free trade is increased competition—that is, independent firms competing to keep prices low and quality high. But as global corporations carry out trade among their own units, such benefits are seldom passed on to consumers.

Percentage of U.S.-parent company trade that is intra-firm [2]

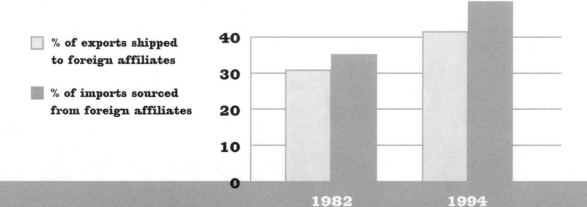

- % of exports shipped to foreign affiliates
- % of imports sourced from foreign affiliates

40
30
20
10
0

1982   1994

B. HIGH TIDE IN THE GLOBAL LABOR POOL

The corporate spread of global assembly lines means that production workers based in richer countries are placed in competition in a global labor pool that includes workers from countries where wages are low and, in most cases, labor rights protections are weak.

1975 The top fifteen exporters of goods in 1975 were almost all richer countries with only slight wage differentials. Of those for which wage data were available, the highest average wage (Sweden, $7.18) was less than two and a half times the lowest average wage (Japan, $3).[3]

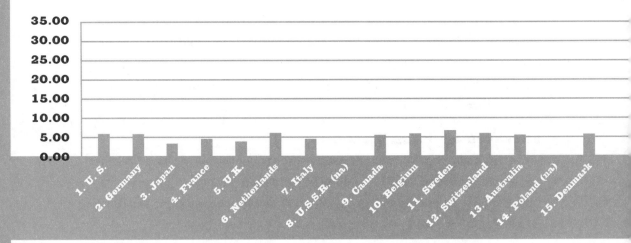

1996 By 1996, the picture had changed dramatically, as five "developing" nations joined the world's top fifteen exporters. The ratio between the highest wage (Germany, $31.87) and the lowest (China, $0.31) was 103 to 1.

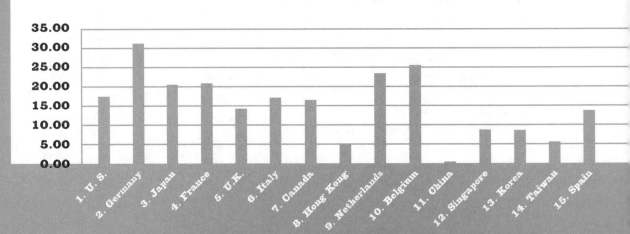

C. COLD WAR MELT

Until the fall of the Berlin Wall in 1989, a sizable share of the world was largely off limits to global corporations based in the West. This included most of China (the world's most populous country), the Soviet Union (which was the world's third most populous nation), Eastern Europe, Vietnam, Cuba, North Korea, and a few other socialist nations. China was quite insulated and exchanged little with the rest of the world, and the others gave incentives for trade and investment with other socialist nations and placed limits on economic exchange with the West. With the collapse of socialism in much of the world, global corporations expanded throughout virtually the entire world. Today, only North Korea remains sealed off to Western investment; Cuba, courtesy of the continued U.S. embargo in trade and investment, remains closed to most U.S. economic transactions.

Coca-Cola, the ultimate symbol of American enterprise, has moved swiftly to dominate the Chinese market

Number of Coca-Cola bottling plants in China in 1979: 0
Number in 1997: 18[4]

Approx. number of Cokes sold in China in 1996: 3 billion[5]

D. OPEN DOORS TO FOREIGN INVESTMENT

Until recently, many nations placed numerous restrictions on foreign investment in certain sectors of their economy. Much of the Third World excluded investment in what they considered "strategic" sectors: mining, petroleum, banking, insurance, and culture. The trade negotiations of the 1990s began to limit the ability of governments to maintain many of these controls. The North American Free Trade Agreement (NAFTA) broke down most barriers to investment in North America. The "trade-related investment measures" (TRIMS) section of the new World Trade Organization accomplished much of the same globally. A flurry of government "privatization" of state-owned enterprises followed, with most buyers coming from the ranks of global corporations. In 1995, governments of the richer nations began negotiating a "Multilateral Agreement on Investments" (MAI) that would, if adopted, remove virtually all remaining restrictions on investment. In 1998, these negotiations stalled indefinitely (see p. 83).

Interested investors can browse magazine ads, like these from *Latin Trade*, for bargains on buying up state-owned enterprise.

Sector	Project	Description	Deadline	Institution	Contact	Phone	Fax
AIRPORTS							
Colombia	Alfonso Bonilla Aragón Airport	Concession for the maintenance and operation of the terminal, runway and ramp.	Pending	AEROCIVIL	Felipe Gutierrez	[57](1)413.1991	[57](1)413.8251
Mexico	Privatization of 35 airports	Includes 9 airports in the southeast region, 13 in the northcenter, 12 in the Pacific and the Benito Juárez International Airport in Mexico City. Bids started in July 1998.	Pending	Secretariat of Communications and Transport	Jorge Silberstein	[52](5)538.5561	[52](5)530.1190
BANKING							
Venezuela	Privatization of Banco de Fomento Regional de los Andes	80% of the bank is up for sale. Bids to start by IIIQ of 1998.	Pending	Venezuelan Investment Fund	Director of Privatizations	[58](2)505.8526	[58](2)505.8521
ENERGY							
Brazil	Privatization of CEAL	The distribution company is up for sale. Bids to start IVQ of 1998.	Pending	BNDES	Jose Pio Borges	[55](21)277.7059	[55](21)533.1538
Brazil	Privatization of CELPE	The distribution company is up for sale. Bids to start IVQ of 1998.	Pending	BNDES	Jose Pio Borges	[55](21)277.7059	[55](21)533.1538
Brazil	Privatization of CEMAR	The distribution company is up for sale. Bids to start IQ of 1999.	Pending	BNDES	Jose Pio Borges	[55](21)277.7059	[55](21)533.1538
Brazil	Privatization of CEPISA	100% of ordinary shares of the company are up for sale. Bids to start IQ of 1999.	Pending	BNDES	Jose Pio Borges	[55](21)277.7059	[55](21)533.1538
Brazil	Privatization of CERON	The distribution company is up for sale. Bids to start IQ of 1999.	Pending	BNDES	Jose Pio Borges	[55](21)277.7059	[55](21)533.1538
Brazil	Privatization of ELETRO-ACRE	The distribution company is up for sale. Bids to start IQ of 1999.	Pending	BNDES	Jose Pio Borges	[55](21)277.7059	[55](21)533.1538
Brazil	Privatization of Gerasul	42% of the generation company is	8/28/98	BNDES	Jose Pio Borges	[55](21)277.7059	[55](21)533.1538

E. GLOBAL FINANCIAL CASINO

Money now moves around the world at a speed that defies and baffles government regulators. Policies to "liberalize" (lift barriers to) investment, combined with advancements in information technology, have facilitated the explosion of private financial flows described earlier and allow about $1.5 trillion a day to travel across borders as foreign-exchange transactions. Only one to two percent of these transactions are related to trade or foreign direct investment. The remainder is for speculation or short-term investments that are subject to rapid flight when investors' perceptions change.[6]

After Mexico suffered a rapid exodus of capital in late 1994, the International Monetary Fund (IMF) and other global agencies claimed that they had set in place new safeguards to prevent a repeat. Yet, over these same years, the IMF and the U.S. Treasury Department were pressuring nations to remove remaining restrictions on inflows and outflows of finance and investment. The rapid flight of short-term capital from Thailand, Malaysia, Indonesia, and South Korea in late 1997, and in Russia and Brazil in 1998, revealed that dozens of other countries are Mexico-style crises waiting to happen as nervous investors move their money elsewhere at the touch of a computer key.

Daily International Foreign Exchange Transactions ($ billions)

	1989	1992	1995	1997

F. IMMIGRANTS NEED NOT APPLY

People have long moved across borders in search of a better life, and tensions between natives and newcomers have always existed. What is new are the extreme measures that governments are taking to keep foreigners out. In the United States, funding for border patrol and related programs more than doubled between 1993 and 1997 as the government invested in hi-tech surveillance equipment, and doubled the number of border agents. Forced to cross the border in more dangerous terrain, an estimated 350 Mexicans died while trying to enter the United States illegally in 1998, four times as many as in 1997. Likewise in Europe, governments have used the excuse of high unemployment to beef up border controls and tighten immigration restrictions, particularly against the unskilled.

HELP WANTED

Is cold weather getting you down and making it impossible to enjoy the great outdoors? Are you looking for a job with more action? Well, the border patrol will hire nearly 2,000 agents in 1998 to be stationed along the Southwest border!

— *text from an actual job notice*
by the Border Patrol

G. THE BIOTECH CRUSADES [7]

For 12,000 years, farmers have survived by saving, breeding, and exchanging seeds for next year's harvest. The health and sustenance of billions of the world's poor depends on the biological diversity that has evolved from these processes. Today, the rise of a new industry called biotechnology threatens to kill that diversity. Chemical, agribusiness, and pharmaceutical companies have manipulated genetic codes to create inventions that supposedly improve upon Mother Nature. In agriculture, corporations are aggressively marketing genetically engineered seeds that are designed to produce higher yields but have raised a number of concerns:

- **MONOPOLIES:** Biotech firms are using strong-arm tactics to gain even more control over the world's food supply and wipe out biodiversity;

- **ENVIRONMENT:** Genetically engineered crops are untested and could spread pesticide-resistant genes to weeds; and

- **HEALTH:** Little research has been done on the effects of eating genetically engineered crops.

The leading biotech giant is U.S.-based Monsanto, which has been on a corporate buying spree since 1996. If the U.S. Justice Department allows all the acquisitions to go through, Monsanto will control over four-fifths of the U.S. cotton seed market and almost half the soybean and corn seed markets. Monsanto also has a strong global presence, with 42 percent of 1997 sales outside the United States.

Monsanto claims that it takes about a decade and $300 million in investment to create a successful genetically engineered seed. To recoup these costs, the company pressures farmers to buy large quantities each year by making them agree not to replant the seeds in the next season. Still, enforcement is difficult, so Monsanto will soon be mar-

keting a package of genes known as "Terminator." When inserted into seeds, the "Terminator" ensures they will never generate seeds of their own.

Monsanto's power to intimidate became dramatically clear in October 1998, when *The Ecologist* magazine devoted an entire issue to a critique of the company.[8] The magazine's printer for twenty-five years informed the editors that it didn't want to print the issue for fear of a libel suit from Monsanto. When the editors found another printer, three wholesalers said they didn't want to distribute the issue because of similar fears. Undeterred, the editors got the magazine out and it has become a key resource for a growing global citizens campaign against Monsanto.

III. Globalization Claims

Since the onset of the debate over the North American Free Trade Agreement
(NAFTA) in 1990, the U.S. public, press, and government have engaged
a lively and often polarized debate over economic globalization.
Almost all participants in the debate admit that corporate-driven globalization
produces winners and losers. Yet there are vast differences in the overall
calculations of winners and losers. Virtually all large corporations claim
that the benefits of such policies far outweigh the losses.
Given the tremendous corporate influence on politics and the increasingly
concentrated corporate ownership of mainstream media,
it should come as little surprise that pro-globalization arguments receive
broad and often unchallenged exposure. This imbalance helped
push NAFTA through Congress in 1993, and a recent survey reveals that
mainstream journalists continue to overwhelmingly favor free trade.

Gap in Media Coverage

- In coverage of the NAFTA debate, the *New York Times* and *Washington Post*
  quoted promoters of the agreement three times as often as critics,
  according to Fairness & Accuracy In Reporting (FAIR).[1]
- Six months before the vote, the *New York Times* ran a special advertising
  section on NAFTA. Two unions opposed to the trade pact tried to buy
  space in the section but were denied.[2]
- A 1998 survey showed that 24 percent of Washington-based journalists
  believe NAFTA expansion is one of the nation's top few priorities,
  compared to only 7 percent of the general public.[3]

Flexing Their Muscle

Despite their formidable power, the pro–free trade forces lost a U.S. legislative battle for the first time in 1997 when Congress failed to pass "fast-track" trade negotiating authority for the Clinton administration. In response, corporate-backed groups have stepped up efforts to influence public and political opinion.

One such group, the Virtual Trade Mission (VTM), has launched a campaign to convince middle school, high school, and college students of the benefits of free trade. VTM shows students slickly produced videos and encourages them to imagine themselves as CEOs of major export firms. Although the group claims to provide a balanced perspective, it gives short shrift to labor and environmental issues. The Business Roundtable, U.S. Chamber of Commerce, and numerous conservative think tanks have also launched ambitious educational campaigns. As we have examined their materials, we see a number of assertions repeated over and over. This section addresses ten of the most common claims.

Gap in political influence[4]

PAC, soft money and individual contributions in $ millions

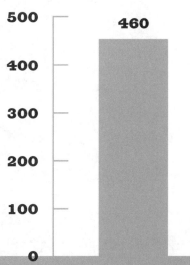

The Corporate Lobby

In July 1998, a lobbyist for Procter & Gamble told the staff of Rep. Bob Ney (R-OH) that P&G contributions to Ney's campaign would depend on his position on fast-track. Ney responded with a letter to the firm's CEO:

I find it appalling that a member of your organization would attempt to influence my vote with political contributions. Also unacceptable was the comment... that somehow my constituents were "not educated" and "do not understand" trade issues. Considering the thousands of working families in the region of Ohio I represent who have lost their jobs because of irrational trade policies, I take personal offense to those comments.

Businesses outspent labor unions (key opponents of corporate globalization policies) 12 to 1 in the 1997/98 election cycle.

CLAIM #1

INCREASED TRADE = MORE JOBS AT HIGHER WAGES

Trade, particularly exports, means more jobs for Americans and better pay.— Business Roundtable

Invisible Export Jobs

U.S. government and corporate officials repeatedly claim that jobs in the export sector pay more than jobs on average. Hence, they argue, expanding exports should be a centerpiece of U.S. policy.

There are several problems with this rationale. In today's state-of-the-art factories, companies can boost productivity and thus increase exports without hiring more employees. Caterpillar, for example, had record exports worth $5.5 billion from its U.S. plants in 1996, even though the firm had cut its U.S. workforce by about one-quarter during the previous three years. At the same time, the company used its global power to withstand a prolonged dispute with U.S. unions.

We have to be globally competitive and that's why we're taking this stand.
—Caterpillar CEO Don Fites, commenting on the company's bitter contract fight with the United Auto Workers, which ended in 1998 after more than six years marked by strikes and lockouts.[5]

Even When Exports Do Support New Jobs, Do They Make Up for Job Losses from Imports?

U.S. trade involves firms exporting goods and services to other countries ($931 billion worth in 1998) as well as importing from the rest of the world ($1,100 billion in 1998).[6] Both exports and imports have been growing rapidly over the past generation as U.S. firms shift goods and parts among their factories around the world. Free trade advocates often boast about jobs created by growing U.S. exports, while ignoring the jobs lost to increased imports. But there's no denying that if consumers switch from buying a U.S.-made product to one made somewhere else, this does result in lost U.S. jobs and poorer quality jobs. This has become a major concern as the U.S. trade deficit has grown for seven consecutive years.

Moreover, even though it is true that export jobs pay better than the average job, so do jobs in industries that face intense import competition. This is because both export and import jobs are usually in manufacturing, while the average job is in the lower-paying service sector.

The Economic Policy Institute compared the industries where exports and imports are growing most rapidly.[7] They found wages are actually higher in those industries where import competition is growing than in those industries where exports are growing fastest (such as agriculture and services). Hence, if we continue with our current policies, trade liberalization will destroy more good jobs in the years ahead.

Imports are damaging wages more than exports are raising them

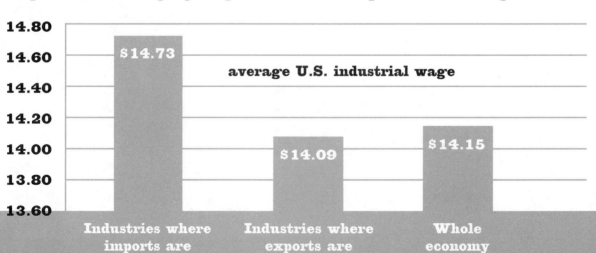

average U.S. industrial wage

	Industries where imports are growing rapidly	Industries where exports are growing rapidly	Whole economy
Wage	$14.73	$14.09	$14.15

Who Is Hurt Most by Trade-Related Job Loss?

One gauge of U.S. job loss related to trade is the NAFTA Transitional Adjustment Assistance (NAFTA-TAA) program, which provides retraining and other benefits to workers whom the government certifies as having lost their jobs because of a shift in production to or increased imports from Mexico or Canada. By early 1999, after five years of NAFTA, the U.S. Department of Labor had certified over 200,000 workers for NAFTA-TAA. These figures do not reflect the total number of jobs lost under NAFTA, but provide a rough picture of who has been hit hardest by trade-related layoffs:[8]

WOMEN

The two industries with the most NAFTA-TAA layoffs are electronics and apparel. Women make up 40 percent of electronics workers and 71 percent of apparel workers, while comprising only thirty-two percent of the U.S. workforce.

PEOPLE OF COLOR

African Americans and Latinos make up slightly less than 20 percent of the U.S. workforce but they comprise nearly 40 percent of apparel workers. Moreover, once they lose their jobs, people of color are more likely than whites to face a pay cut in their new jobs.[9]

RURAL COMMUNITIES

Only about 21 percent of the U.S. population is rural, but rural workers represent about 40 percent of U.S. workers certified for NAFTA-TAA. Because of few alternative employment opportunities, particularly because of the decline in family farming, these workers are often forced to uproot and move to another area in search of work.

But What About the American Job Machine?

Free traders dismiss trade-related job loss by pointing to the overall low U.S. unemployment rate. Indeed, the United States has experienced tremendous job growth during the past decade. The big question is "what kind of jobs?"

The Labor Department reports that only about 35 percent of dislocated workers find new jobs that pay as well or better than their old ones.[10] This is because the jobs available are often undesirable. The Economic Policy Institute has found that nearly 30 percent of Americans are now employed in "nonstandard" work arrangements, which includes all those that are not permanent, full-time jobs. On average, such jobholders earn less, are less likely to receive health insurance and pensions, and face greater insecurity than full-time workers in standard jobs, even when they have the same level of education and experience. Because they hold the majority of all nonstandard positions, women and people of color are hurt most by the lack of equity in wages and benefits.

And in the future? Labor Department projections indicate that the number one growth occupation is cashier, which in 1996 paid on average $6.58 per hour. The only full-time workers paid *less* than cashiers are restaurant staff, shampooers in hair salons, amusement park attendants, ushers, and bellhops.

Globalization Blackmail

Americans who manage to maintain jobs in manufacturing must contend with employers who often use their increased mobility against the workers' interests. An extensive study of organizing drives at U.S. manufacturing firms by Cornell University found that in 62 percent of the cases, management fought the union by threatening to shut down the plant and move production to a lower-wage area.[11]

Examples of employer intimidation tactics:

- attaching shipping labels with a Mexican address to equipment throughout the plant;
- posting maps of North America with an arrow pointing from the current plant site to Mexico;
- letters directly stating that the company would have to shut down if the union won the election.

Workers and union officials report that the same tactics are common in bargaining sessions and when individual employees request raises. The blackmail factor at least partly explains why U.S. wages have been stagnant for most of the 1990s despite record corporate profits and record low unemployment. U.S. workers did receive a slight increase in real wages in 1998, but pay is still not as high as in 1989.

CLAIM #2

AS TRADE SPURS ECONOMIC GROWTH, GOVERNMENTS INVEST MORE IN THE ENVIRONMENT

An open world trading system contributes to the prosperity of less developed countries and helps them get to the point of mandating and enforcing environmental standards similar to those in the developed world.

—Gene Grossman, Princeton University, whose work was often cited in the NAFTA debate[12]

Developing Country Growth Often Based on Resource Plunder

Globalization puts multiple pressures on the environment. The rapid shift of factories to China, Indonesia, Mexico, and elsewhere has vastly increased pollution around the world. Some companies deliberately choose production locations where enforcement of environmental rules is lax and take advantage of the government's inattention to pollute in ways that would be unacceptable in their home countries. Further, the World Bank and International Monetary Fund pressure countries to pay off loans through increased export earnings. This often means cutting down forest for timber exports or plantation expansion, depleting fishing stocks, or expanding open-pit mines.

Free traders counter that expanded exports fuel economic growth which, in turn, gives governments more resources to invest in environmental clean-up. The record, however, suggests otherwise. All three leading recipients of new investment in the developing world—China, Mexico, and Indonesia—are becoming environmental nightmares.

CHINA *1996 Rank in Developing World in:*

EXPORTS: 1 ($151 billion)[13]   PRIVATE INVESTMENT: 1 ($52 billion)[14]

Since 1980, China has enjoyed soaring exports and the world's highest economic growth rate, but the country has quickly become one of the world's most polluted countries.

- Coal consumption has doubled and poor treatment methods have contributed to an increase in acid rain levels of up to 90 percent and a lung disease epidemic.[15]
- At least five of the ten cities with the world's worst air pollution are in China.[16]
- Despite international opposition from environmentalists, China is building the world's largest hydroelectric dam to meet industrial energy demands.

MEXICO *1996 Rank in Developing World in:*

EXPORTS: 3 ($95 billion)   PRIVATE INVESTMENT: 2 ($28.1 billion)

The explosion of factories (*maquiladoras*) has intensified environmental problems on both sides of the U.S.–Mexico border, while foreign investment in natural resource sectors threatens the country's biodiversity and the livelihoods of indigenous peoples.

- Sewage-contaminated water spreads gastrointestinal diseases that are now the leading killer of Mexican border children. On the U.S. side, contamination is blamed for hepatitis A rates three times the national average.
- Maquiladora workers often face environmental hazards, such as an unexplained gas leak that hospitalized 226 Alcoa workers in Ciudad Acuna in 1994.
- Since 1994, 15 U.S. wood products companies have set up operations in Mexico, primarily in regions with some of the continent's largest remaining forests.[17]

INDONESIA *1996 Rank in Developing World in:*

EXPORTS: 6 ($49.7 billion)   PRIVATE INVESTMENT: 3 ($17.9 billion)

Indonesia, fueled by oil reserves, grew rapidly over the past three decades under the tight control of the dictator Suharto. Suharto parceled out access to the nation's abundant forests, plantation lands, and gold mines to his children and cronies who formed links with global corporations to plunder them for export.

- Indonesia is second only to Brazil in the annual rate of tropical rainforest destruction.[18]
- As Suharto clung to power in his final months in office, he agreed to IMF demands to expand palm oil plantations, a move that added pressure on tropical forests to make way for plantations.

Globalization Also Threatens the Environment in Developed Countries

BLACKMAIL Mobile corporations can more effectively use threats of moving production elsewhere in order to weaken U.S. environmental regulations. For example, an official of Boise Cascade, a timber giant that had already moved some of its mills from the United States to Mexico, made this thinly veiled threat in the midst of a congressional debate over logging rights:

The number of timber sales [granted by the government] will determine our decision to move south.[19]

This kind of intimidation helped the logging industry pressure Congress into passing a law in 1995 to allow increased logging and to suspend environmental protections in national forests.

LAWS OVERTURNED Environmental laws are also subject to being challenged under free trade rules as "unfair barriers to trade."

In 1998, the government of Canada caved in to pressure from a U.S. corporation to rescind a law prohibiting the import of MMT, a fuel additive believed to cause nervous system damage to workers exposed to relatively high levels. Auto manufacturers also charge that MMT damages auto emission control systems. U.S.-based Ethyl Corporation, the producer of MMT (formally, *methylcyclopentadieny manganese tricarbonyl*) challenged the ban, both in court and under NAFTA, claiming lost profits. Fearful of losing a high-profile NAFTA ruling, the Canadian government agreed to repeal the ban, pay Ethyl $13 million in damages, and publicly state that MMT does not pose a health threat, despite mounting evidence to the contrary.[20]

FOREIGN INVESTMENT AUTOMATICALLY RAISES LIVING STANDARDS

The injection of U.S. capital and technology ... creates jobs and a better standard of living for both [the United States and the recipient country].
—George Munoz, CEO, Overseas Private Investment Corporation [21]

Most developing-country governments are pursuing aggressive strategies to attract foreign investment by offering low taxes, repressed workforces, and lax enforcement of regulations. Many governments have received strong pressure from the World Bank and IMF to move in this direction with the promise that increased investment will bring growth and higher living standards. In a few countries, increased foreign investment has indeed corresponded with rising wages. However, without strong protections for workers and citizens, there is no guarantee that foreign investment will benefit the average person.

Mexico: No Payoff Without Rights

The amount of foreign direct investment into Mexico jumped from less than $3 billion per year in the 1980s to $11 billion in 1998.[22] And yet the impact of all this money on Mexican workers has been mixed, at best. Yes, some jobs have been created, but real wages are actually worth *less* today than in the 1980s. Between 1987 and 1998, the earning power of the minimum wage declined by seventy-two percent.[23]

Moreover, the country has experienced an overall decline in employment. In the manufacturing sector this has been primarily because of bankruptcies among locally-owned firms crippled by high interest rates the government has set to attract foreign investors.[24]

This Favesa factory in Ciudad Juarez, owned by U.S.-based Lear Seating, is an example of the foreign investment that has flooded into Mexico. More than 3,000 plants on the Mexican side of the border now produce goods for export to the United States. Favesa stiches automotive seat covers for Ford Motor Company.

The Favesa plant's modern appearance contrasts sharply with the housing in which employees live. Pablo Yermo, who earns about $59 for a sixty-hour workweek at Favesa, lives in a shack made of card-board and wood scraps. His dusty plot, which lacks water and sewage services, is shared by two children and seven adults, five of whom work at Favesa.

photos: George McAlmon

Nigeria: No $ for Oil

Billions of dollars in foreign oil money have had little impact on Nigeria except to prop up an unaccountable government and pollute the lands around the oil fields. Meanwhile, average Nigerians have watched their living standards decline, as per capita income fell from $1,560 in 1992 to $1,270 in 1995.

Nigerian activist Ken Saro Wiwa spoke out against the oil giants for extracting his nation's resources while leaving little behind except environmental ruin. The military government retaliated by arresting him on flimsy charges of inciting violence and executed him in 1995 along with eight other activists.

Nigeria [25]

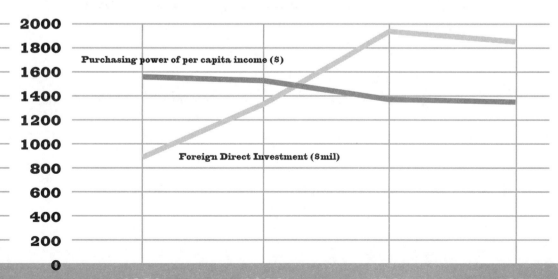

Purchasing power of per capita income ($)

Foreign Direct Investment ($mil)

| 1992 | 1993 | 1994 | 1997 |

CLAIM
#4

FREE TRADE IS THE CONSUMERS' BEST FRIEND

[Increased trade] spurs innovation among domestic firms while protecting consumers from potential monopolies.
—Daniel Griswold, Cato Institute[26]

That consumers benefit from freer trade is perhaps the most pervasive assertion of globalization supporters. And there is no question that globalization has expanded the variety of goods available in the marketplace. Pristine malls selling the same goods now tower over cityscapes from Manila to Mexico City.

It is also true that roughly a third of U.S. imports come from poorer nations where workers earn a fraction of U.S. wages. Hence, these goods often *enter* the United States at prices far below the price of U.S.-made goods. Yet, a key question is how often firms then *sell* those goods to consumers at lower prices versus how often they hike the prices and keep the benefits of trade for themselves.

Evidence suggests that in sectors of the economy where many small producers compete, such as clothing production, consumers *may* find that increased trade lowers prices. However, in sectors where a handful of huge global firms dominate the market for a particular product, such as automobiles, international trade often does not result in lower prices.

Many industries are dominated by a few giant firms

Percentage of global sales controlled by top five firms in each sector: [27]

60%	autos
>50%	electronics
>30%	airlines, aerospace, steel, oil, personal computers, chemicals, media

No Free Trade Bargains at General Motors

General Motors demonstrates how global firms that dominate a particular industry can monopolize the benefits of international trade. In 1994, GM decided to expand production of its popular "Suburban" sport utility vehicle. But instead of investing in its Suburban plant in Janesville, Wisconsin, or adding capacity at another U.S. plant, the company built a new facility in Silao, Mexico, which began producing Suburbans for the U.S. market. Yet, as GM's wage bill plummeted, the price of Suburbans sold in the United States continued to rise.[28]

GM's move to Mexico drastically cut the firm's labor costs ...

Avg. 1996 wages of workers who make Suburbans:

U.S. $18.96 p/hr.   Mexico $1.54 p/hr.

... yet GM did not lower the price of the vehicle

Sticker price of Suburban:

1994: $21,000–$24,500   1996: $23,500–$31,000

By 1996, GM produced nearly as many Suburbans in Silao, Mexico (80,400), as in Janesville, Wisconsin (83,000).

GLOBALIZATION LIFTS ALL BOATS

CLAIM #5

Free Trade Helps Lift World Poor—headline, *Washington Post*

The World Bank argues that accelerated globalization has coincided with greater world equality, pointing out that developing countries as a whole are growing faster than the major industrial nations.[29] However, during the period of rapid globalization of the 1980s and 1990s, the gap between rich and poor within most nations has widened. Aside from the ten to twelve fastest growing developing nations, the rest of the developing world is not catching up with the richer nations. Worldwide growth has also slowed—to about two percent a year in the 1990s, compared to three percent a year in the 1980s.[30] Indeed, with a handful of exceptions, most countries in the world have experienced an increase in economic inequality over the past fifteen years.

Inequality Within Countries:

UN and World Bank studies indicate that economic liberalization has been accompanied by greater wage inequality in the following developing and former communist countries:[31]

Argentina	Estonia	Lithuania	Slovakia
Belarus	Ethiopia	Mexico	Slovenia
Bulgaria	Ghana	Moldova	Taiwan
Chile	Hong Kong	Nigeria	Tanzania
China	Hungary	Philippines	Turkmenistan
Czech Republic	Kazakhstan	Poland	Ukraine
Dominican Republic	Kirgiz Republic	Romania	Uruguay
Ecuador	Latvia	Russia	Uzbekistan

Inequality has also risen in the following industrialized countries:

Australia	Germany	Netherlands	United States
Belgium	Japan	Sweden	United Kingdom

Inequality between countries:

• The gap in per capita income between the industrial and developing worlds tripled from 1960 to 1993.[32]

Inequality between Haves and Have-Nots:

• By 1999, the wealth of the world's 475 billionaires was greater than the combined incomes of the poorest half of humanity.[33]

HOW GLOBALIZATION IS PULLING US APART

Dragging the bottom down

IN THE UNITED STATES: Low-income workers, including large numbers of people of color and women, have seen their real wages erode. Though the wage gap narrowed slightly in 1998, average real wages were still lower than in 1989.[34] Even some free trade proponents admit that twenty to twenty-five percent of the increase in inequality may be due to globalization, specifically because of import competition from low-wage countries and employers taking advantage of a larger pool of low-wage labor, either by moving (or threatening to move) to developing countries or hiring recent immigrants.[35]

IN DEVELOPING COUNTRIES: Trade and investment liberalization, as part of overall restructuring programs, have increased poverty as governments have slashed funding for food and other social programs and promoted export-oriented agriculture. Between 1987 and 1993, overall poverty increased in sub-Saharan Africa, Latin America, the Caribbean, and the former Soviet Union, and Eastern Europe. The latter's deterioration has been most dramatic, with the percentage living in poverty rising from 4 to 45 percent.[36]

Boosting the top

IN THE UNITED STATES: Executives of large corporations have enjoyed skyrocketing compensation as corporate profits, buoyed by success in global markets, have soared. Top executives enjoyed a 36 percent pay hike in 1998, taking in on average $10.6 million—419 times that of an average factory worker.[37]

IN DEVELOPING COUNTRIES: In 1996, Asia (excluding Japan) and Latin America boasted 121 of the world's 447 billionaires. Ten years previous, only one Latin American and four Asians outside Japan made the cut.[38] Many have obtained their wealth by snatching up state-owned industries at bargain rates when governments were forced to privatize.

WHAT'S GOOD FOR GENERAL MOTORS IS GOOD FOR THE REST OF US

CLAIM #6

What is good for the country is good for General Motors and what's good for General Motors is good for the country.
—General Motors CEO Charles Wilson, testimony before Senate Armed Forces Committee, 1952

Corporate leaders often use a variation of Wilson's famous argument when urging public support for free trade policies. They claim that lifting barriers to trade and investment will make companies more competitive and profitable, and that these profits will trickle down to the rest of us. In Wilson's day, this argument carried some weight, because large U.S. corporations contributed far more to U.S. society through taxes and jobs than they do today. By contrast, global firms now have little national loyalty. While ever more influential politically, they provide a declining share of government revenues and jobs and are increasingly difficult for governments to regulate.

Declining Tax Burden

The most powerful U.S. corporations have combined geographic mobility with political clout to minimize their tax obligations. Since 1960, the share of federal tax revenues paid by corporations has dropped by more than half. This is partly due to a practice among many corporations with far-flung operations of simply recording profits in jurisdictions with low tax rates.

Share of federal taxes paid by corporations [39]

25%	
20%	23.2%
15%	
10%	11.4%
5%	
0%	
1960	1998

Cutting Jobs While Boosting Sales

The top ten U.S. manufacturing firms employ far fewer people today than they did thirty years ago, despite soaring revenues. Since 1968, worldwide employment at these firms has dropped 33 percent, while sales (adjusted for inflation) have climbed 94 percent.[40] Much of the drop in employment reflects technological advancements that automated certain jobs. This is not always a negative development, especially in the case of jobs that were dangerous or otherwise undesirable. However, the basic point remains that leading firms have increased their economic and political clout while contributing less to society in jobs and tax revenues.

Top 10 U.S. Manufacturing Companies

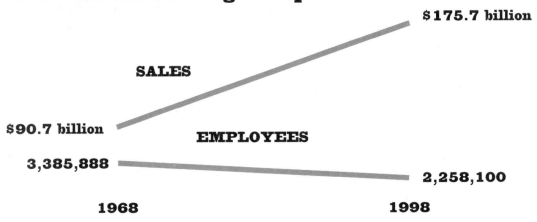

SALES

$175.7 billion

$90.7 billion

EMPLOYEES

3,385,888

2,258,100

1968   1998

ranked by 1998 sales	1968 employees	1998 employees	1968 sales ($1000)	1998 sales (1968 $1000)	employment % change	sales % change
General Motors	757,231	601,500	22,755,403	33,315,779	-21	46
Ford Motor	415,039	345,200	14,075,100	29,825,692	-17	112
Exxon•	151,000	79,500	14,091,337	20,796,572	-47	48
General Electric	400,000	284,500	8,381,633	20,749,484	-29	148
IBM	241,974	280,200	6,888,549	16,866,378	16	145
Philip Morris	314,496	148,000	675,408	11,939,901	-53	1,668
Boeing	142,400	234,500	3,273,980	11,597,274	65	254
AT&T	872,018	119,300	14,100,014	11,067,328	-86	-22
Mobil	78,300	42,100	6,220,996	9,846,758	-46	58
Hewlett Packard	13,430	123,300	268,849	9,719,331	818	3,515
Total	3,385,888	2,258,100	$90,731,269	$175,724,494	-33	94

•was Standard Oil of NJ

CLAIM #7

IT'S FINE THAT POORER NATIONS PRODUCE GOODS IN SWEATSHOPS; THE UNITED STATES DEVELOPED THAT WAY

My concern is not that there are too many sweatshops [in developing countries] but that there are too few. —Jeffrey Sachs, Harvard University [41]

For centuries, much of the world's manufacturing came from small facilities with dismal health and safety conditions where workers (often children) earned less than a poverty wage working long hours. Such facilities have earned the name sweatshops. Some economists claim that such plants are an essential step toward prosperity for developing countries, pointing to the brutal working conditions that characterized much of early U.S. industrial development. However, while such exploitative practices might help corporations increase profits, they are not an inevitable element of a healthy development strategy.

There is more evidence that it was the struggles against sweatshops, not the sweatshops themselves, that led to improved working conditions in the United States. Many labor union activists lost their lives or made other tremendous sacrifices to win the struggle for the minimum wage, forty-hour work week and other protections. Unfortunately today, as clothing retailers roam the globe looking for the most exploited workforces, once again the United States is plagued by sweatshops. The U.S. General Accounting Office estimates that there are as many as 7,000 garment industry sweatshops in New York City, Los Angeles, Miami, El Paso, and New Orleans alone. Sweatshops can trap workers in a vicious cycle of malnourishment, poor educational opportunities, and dangerous working conditions. This leads to more poverty and inequality, rather than laying the foundation for building a strong, empowered middle class and a viable democracy.

"If we pay them starvation wages— why do they need a lunch break?"

Nike on the Run

Footwear giant Nike is a prime example of a globe-trotting company constantly on the run in search of the lowest possible wages. In some cases, countries with sweatshops that produced goods for Nike and other companies experienced a rise in living standards. However, the improvements had more to do with the host governments' strategic industrial policies and the struggles of workers than sweatshop jobs.[42]

1967: Nike began manufacturing in Japan, with some limited production in the United States.

1972: When Japanese wages began improving, Nike took off for South Korea and Taiwan.

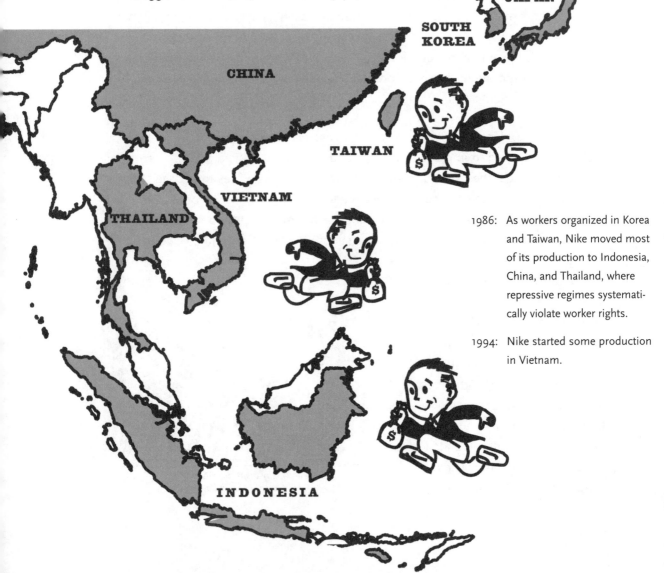

1986: As workers organized in Korea and Taiwan, Nike moved most of its production to Indonesia, China, and Thailand, where repressive regimes systematically violate worker rights.

1994: Nike started some production in Vietnam.

CLAIM #8

IMMIGRANTS ARE A DRAIN ON THE U.S. ECONOMY

America is for Americans.
—former Presidential candidate Bob Dole[43]

There are as many misconceptions about the *negative* impacts of the flow of people across borders as there are myths about the *benefits* of trade and investment flows. Often, the same people who champion the rights of U.S. corporations to operate freely abroad also scapegoat immigrants in the United States for draining social programs, stealing jobs, and dragging down wages.

Welfare Costs vs. Taxes Paid

The National Academy of Sciences calculated the taxes a U.S. immigrant and his or her descendants are likely to pay over their lifetimes and then subtracted the cost of the government services they're likely to use. The result: each additional immigrant and his or her descendants will provide $80,000 in extra tax revenues over their lifetimes.[44] Likewise, the Urban Institute calculated that all immigrants arriving in the United States between 1970 and 1992 paid taxes that outstripped their costs for welfare and other social services during this period by $25 to $30 billion.

U.S. 1997 federal government expenditures ($ million)

Anti-immigrant measures (including border patrols, investigations and intelligence, detention and deportation, and construction of barriers) are popular in Washington. In fact, they receive far more taxpayer money than some key programs to build workers' skills in the United States or to fight hunger in the Third World.[45]

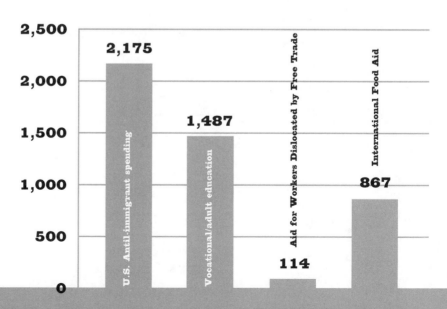

Employment: A Non-Issue

A number of respected studies, using a variety of methods, indicate that immigration does not have a significant effect on overall U.S. employment. The explanation is that new entrants not only *fill* jobs, they also *create* jobs through their purchasing power and by starting new businesses. In fact, one study showed that states with relatively small immigrant populations had higher unemployment rates than those with a larger immigrant presence.

Wages: Affluent Gain, Poor Lose

The National Academy of Sciences concludes that there are no negative effects of immigration on most American workers, with one important exception—the very low-skilled. Workers with less than a high school degree (about 15 percent of the workforce) earn about 5 percent less than they would without competition from low-skilled immigrants. Immigration further contributes to the growing disparity between rich and poor by providing benefits to employers, such as owners of large agricultural enterprises or those who hire immigrant domestic workers.

However, the solution to this problem is not to attack immigration. According to the UNITE apparel union, "the best way to help America's low wage workers is to stick to the basics: improved wages, improved health care, and reform of our labor laws so that all workers—immigrant and native born—can freely join unions and protect their rights."[46]

INS Raids

In the name of U.S. job protection, the Immigration and Naturalization Service (INS) raids workplaces in search of undocumented workers. The positive effect of these tactics is dubious.

For example, the INS's 1982 "Operation Jobs" involved raids in eight cities that led to the deportation of 6,000 workers. The result? Sales plummeted at neighborhood businesses that catered to Latinos. The few Americans who took the vacated jobs quit within days because of brutal conditions. Two weeks after the raids, the press reported that the deportees were once again at work.

Despite such fiascoes, the INS has stepped up such raids in recent years, often inadvertently snaring U.S. citizens who happen to have dark skin. In one raid of a Wyoming ski resort, the INS reportedly carted detainees away in horse trailers.[47]

Undocumented workers arrested in INS workplace raids [48]

Year	Workers arrested
1988	3,642
1990	8,942
1992	10,595
1994	10,273
1996	13,848
1997	19,040

TRADE = DEMOCRACY

By expanding trade, we can advance the cause of freedom and democracy around the world.
—President Bill Clinton, State of the Union address, 1997

A cornerstone of U.S. foreign policy in the 1990s is the assertion that free trade will bring prosperity, which is the breeding ground of democracy. In most cases, however, increased trade does not go hand in hand with greater freedoms. In its 1997 annual human rights report, the U.S. State Department reveals that many countries with export growth rates well above the world average during the 1990s are far from free societies.[49] Because free trade policies often widen the gap between rich and poor, they also increase social tensions in countries and poison the ground for democratic development.

The State Department identified the following forms of abuse as significant problems:

High export growth countries	Average annual export growth (1990–1995)	extrajudicial killings	torture	restricted freedoms of speech, religion, or association	government influence over judiciary	excessive force	arbitrary arrest	significant child labor
Thailand	21.6	x	x	x		x		x
Indonesia	21.3	x		x	x			
Sri Lanka	17.0	x	x	x			x	x
Kenya	16.6	x	x	x	x		x	
Mexico	14.7	x	x				x	x
China	14.3		x	x			x	
El Salvador	13.0	x				x	x	
Bangladesh	12.7	x	x	x			x	x
Peru	11.0		x	x	x	x	x	x
Chile	10.5		x			x		
Turkey	8.8		x	x		x		
Pakistan	8.8	x	x	x	x	x	x	x
Tunisia	7.7		x	x	x			
World	6.0							

SUPERIOR PRODUCTIVITY WILL PROTECT U.S. WORKERS FROM GLOBALIZATION

Our working men and women are the most productive of any nation on the face of the earth. You give us the opportunity to sell our products unimpeded... and we'll knock the socks off the workers of any other country in this world.

—Al Gore, debating NAFTA with Ross Perot on "Larry King Live," November 1993

Free trade supporters often accuse their opponents of lacking faith in the superiority of American workers. We needn't worry about firms moving jobs to low-wage countries, they say, because U.S. workers can out-compete anyone. However, this argument overlooks the reality that many corporations are in fact already achieving comparable productivity levels in countries where worker rights are denied, but industrial infrastructure is now quite advanced. With technology and capital goods from global corporations, it should not be surprising that some developing countries can achieve high levels of productivity in select industries. But it is this high productivity in combination with deliberate government action to repress wages and destroy independent unions that leads to skewed development and debilitating competition.

CHINA: NOT JUST A CHEAP SHOEMAKER

China still specializes in making cheap consumer goods, but the country's technological sophistication is also on the rise. In 1997, 26.5 percent of China's exports to the United States comprised machinery (including consumer electrical goods such as telephones and washing machines as well as industrial equipment), up from only 1.6 percent in 1985.[50] China has improved its technological capacity in part by requiring U.S. firms that want to sell products in China to also invest in and transfer technology to that country.

MEXICO: HARDLY A BACKWATER

During the NAFTA debate, supporters often pointed out that overall U.S. productivity was far higher than Mexico's. However, according to auto industry analyst Harley Shaiken, such "overall" figures mask high levels of productivity achieved by individual export plants and the potential for further advances. Ford's Hermosillo assembly plant is a prime example. Three years after this state-of-the-art plant went on line, the Mercury Tracer it produced had the second-highest quality rating for small cars sold in the U.S. market.[51]

IV. Who's Driving Globalization

Marlboro maker Philip Morris sells over 2.6 billion cigarettes each day:
one for every man, woman, and child on earth every two days.
Each cigarette contains a blend of tobacco from as many as seventy nations.
Philip Morris's decisions shape the lives of hundreds of thousands
of tobacco farmers, workers in tobacco warehouses, buyers, shippers,
factory workers, Wall Street financiers, and Madison Avenue advertisers even
before the tens of millions of its consumers light up each morning.

General Motors, Ford, and Chrysler drove the decisions that created
the interstate highway system, the development of suburbs, the atrophy
of public transport, and the development of millions of jobs in related
industries. Indeed, in the United States alone, the major car and truck firms
consume over 60 percent of the oil, 50 percent of the rubber,
65 percent of the iron, 50 percent of the carpeting, and 20 percent
of the electronics and aluminum produced in this country.[1]

These giant firms and their counterparts in other countries are the principal drivers of the world economy. Their decisions shape the lives of most of the world's people and the directions of every national economy. They produce most of the world's goods and services, finance that production, and trade more and more of it across borders. In turn, they have steered the agendas of most governments at every level and have twisted the operations of the global institutions set up to govern the global economy in their interests.

Yet, their activities are generating a massive citizen backlash. This section outlines the two main sets of private actors at the center of the global economy: transnational corporations and transnational banks. We then give an overview of the global public institutions that increasingly serve as a battleground between corporations and citizens. The final section of this book offers a road map to the growing citizen backlash.

A. PRIVATE ACTORS

Corporations

Although it is our public institutions that enact and enforce the rules of the road, large international corporations have been the principal driving force behind globalization.

The power of these global firms has grown in a number of ways. According to the United Nations, there were 7,000 transnational corporations in 1970. Today, there are 44,000, with 280,000 affiliates around the world. Of these, it is the largest 200 firms that are the dominant engines of the global economy.

The Top 200 Firms' Profits and Sales Have Outpaced World Economic Growth

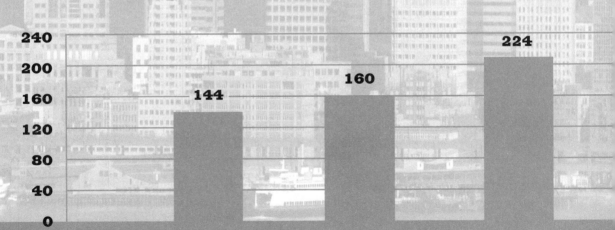

Percent growth (1983–1997)

	World GDP	Sales of top 200 firms	Profits of top 200 firms
	144	160	224

Top 200 Firms

The largest 200 global firms have become so dominant that they have begun to rival nation-states in their economic clout.

- The amount of money spent on cheap underwear and other discount goods at Wal-Mart in 1997 was more than the GDP's of 163 countries.
- The oil-rich nation of Saudi Arabia could not top the sales of six corporations—GM and Ford, Royal Dutch Shell and the Japanese firms Mitsui, Itochu, and Mitsubishi.
- Cigarette-peddler Philip Morris had sales greater than the GDPs of 148 countries.

No more monopoly busting

At the end of World War II, the American occupiers broke up the great business combines of Germany and Japan on the grounds that they were incompatible with democracy. Within the United States, business history is the story of waves of mergers, followed by efforts to control or reverse this trend through legislation. However, since the 1980s, government has taken a hands-off approach. In 1998, the United States witnessed a tremendous merger boom involving deals worth $1.6 trillion, up 78 percent from 1997.[2] In this era of globalization, governments and corporations argue that the mergers are needed for firms to compete in global markets.

Where Are the Jobs?

The Top 200 firms' economic clout far outweighs the benefits they provide in terms of employment [3]

Top 200 Firms

1997 sales as a percentage of world GDP: 26%
1997 employees as a percentage of world's workforce: 0.74%

Corporate vs. Country Economic Clout

The Top 100 [4] (Fifty-one are corporations, only forty-nine are countries)

	Country or Corporation	GDP/sales 1997 ($mil)		Country or Corporation	GDP/sales 1997 ($mil)		Country or Corporation	GDP/sales 1997 ($mil)
1	United States	7,745,705	35	ITOCHU	126,691	69	MOBIL	59,978
2	Japan	4,201,636	36	Saudi Arabia	125,266	70	PHILIP MORRIS	56,114
3	Germany	2,100,110	37	EXXON	122,379	71	ALLIANZ WORLDWIDE	55,397
4	France	1,396,540	38	WAL-MART	119,299	72	SONY	55,058
5	United Kingdom	1,271,710	39	Greece	119,111	73	Czech Republic	54,890
6	Italy	1,145,370	40	Finland	116,170	74	NISSAN MOTOR	53,503
7	China	825,020	41	MARUBENI	111,173	75	AT&T	53,261
8	Brazil	786,466	42	SUMITOMO	102,443	76	FIAT GROUP	52,590
9	Canada	603,085	43	Malaysia	97,523	77	HONDA MOTOR	48,899
10	Spain	531,419	44	Portugal	97,357	78	CREDIT SUISSE	48,641
11	South Korea	442,543	45	Singapore	96,319	79	UNILEVER	48,479
12	Russia Fed.	440,562	46	TOYOTA MOTOR	95,181	80	HSBC CORP	48,404
13	Australia	391,045	47	Israel	91,965	81	NESTLE	48,230
14	Netherlands	360,472	48	GENERAL ELECTRIC	90,840	82	Algeria	45,997
15	India	359,812	49	Colombia	85,202	83	BOEING	45,800
16	Mexico	344,766	50	Philippines	83,125	84	TEXACO	45,187
17	Argentina	322,730	51	NISSHO IWAI	91,932	85	Hungary	44,845
18	Switzerland	293,400	52	IBM	78,508	86	TOSHIBA	44,488
19	Belgium	264,400	53	NIPPON TEL & TEL	77,019	87	Ukraine	44,007
20	Sweden	227,751	54	AXA-UAP	76,869	88	STATE FARM INS.	43,957
21	Indonesia	214,593	55	Egypt	75,482	89	VEBA GROUP	43,866
22	Austria	206,239	56	Chile	74,292	90	ELF AQUITAINE	43,570
23	Turkey	181,464	57	Ireland	72,037	91	TOMEN	43,420
24	GENERAL MOTORS	178,174	58	DAIMLER BENZ	71,536	92	TOKYO ELEC. POWER	43,017
25	Hong Kong	171,401	59	BRITISH PETROLEUM	71,175	93	HEWLETT-PACKARD	42,895
26	Denmark	161,107	60	HITACHI	68,599	94	DUPONT	41,304
27	Thailand	157,263	61	Venezuela	67,316	95	SEARS ROEBUCK	41,296
28	FORD MOTOR	153,627	62	VOLKSWAGEN GROUP	65,306	96	DEUTSCHE BANK	40,778
29	Norway	153,403	63	New Zealand	64,999	97	FUJITSU	40,632
30	MITSUI & CO.	142,754	64	Pakistan	64,360	98	NEC	39,945
31	Poland	135,659	65	MATSHUSHITA ELEC.	64,310	99	PHILIPS GROUP	39,181
32	South Africa	129,094	66	SIEMANS GROUP	63,731	100	DEUTSCHE TELEKOM	38,956
33	MITSUBISHI	128,982	67	Peru	62,431			
34	ROYAL DUTCH/ SHELL GROUP	128,108	68	CHRYSLER	61,147			

The Top 100 Banks and other Sources of Financial Flows

Merger mania has consumed the world's banking industry since the mid-1990s. By 1997, the combined assets of the world's top 100 banks totalled $21.3 trillion, or the equivalent of 73 percent of global economic activity.[5] Unlike the top 200 corporations, the United States is not the dominant force in banking. During the 1930s, the U.S. government enacted legislation that curbed banking expansion across state borders and between commercial and investment banking. Despite the breaking down of some of these walls, there are still thousands of banks in this country. Hence, the top U.S. bank—Chase Manhattan—ranks only number eighteen globally in terms of assets.

Top 10 Global Banks (ranked by 1997 assets)

1. Bank of Tokyo-Mitsubishi (Japan)
2. Deutsche Bank AG (Germany)
3. Sumitomo Bank (Japan)
4. Credit Suisse Group (Switzerland)
5. HSBC Holdings (United Kingdom)
6. Dai-Ichi Kangyo Bank (Japan)
7. Sanwa Bank (Japan)
8. Credit Agricole Mutual (France)
9. Fuji Bank (Japan)
10. ABN-AMRO Bank (Netherlands)

Top 5 U.S. Banks (and 1997 global rank)

1. Chase Manhattan (18)
2. Citicorp (21)
3. Nationsbank (27)
4. JP Morgan (29)
5. Bank America (30)

The world's leading banks are the first to develop new information technologies to speed the flows of their lendable capital around the globe. More and more of their money flits around the world between business enterprises and the well-to-do while their less-privileged customers find it more and more difficult to access affordable credit. For example, Nationsbank's Global Finance division, with offices in twelve foreign countries, was the agent or co-agent for 420 business deals valued at $281.6 billion in 1995.[6] That same year an investigation of the bank's lending practices in four U.S. cities revealed that Nationsbank denied African Americans home loans at least three times more often than whites, and at a rate that far surpassed almost all other major housing lenders.[7]

While often denying small loans to deserving customers in the United States, many U.S. banks have made huge, reckless international loans, aware that they were unlikely to suffer negative consequences. For example, large U.S. banks deserve a good share of the blame for the Asian crisis that began in June 1997 because they had lent a great deal of money to Asian nations without rigorous checks. Six U.S. banks had over $19 billion in loan exposure to Thailand, the Philippines, Indonesia, and Korea at the time the crisis broke.[8] Nevertheless, these banks are doing fine thanks to taxpayers who have financed International Monetary Fund (IMF) bailout funds to these countries. After July 1997, the U.S. Treasury Department worked closely with the IMF to orchestrate massive bailouts to the tune of $121 billion.[9] Much of that money went to repay U.S. and other financial institutions. Moreover, while millions of workers in Asia and elsewhere suffered under the crisis, the CEOs of the banks that made the bad loans fared extremely well in 1997.

Banking CEOs who made bad loans to Asia got big raises

Bank	CEO	1997 salary & bonus	% change from 1996	1997 total compensation (incl. options gains)
BankAmerica	David Coulter	$5,237,500	47.88	$6,681,200
Citicorp	John Reed	$4,000,000	15.38	$4,090,000
Chase Manhattan	Walter Shipley	$6,148,000	8.55	$11,285,000
JP Morgan (Morgan Guaranty)	Douglas A. Warner III	$3,041,667	-5.95	$8,967,667
Bankers Trust	Frank Newman	$10,937,500	22.54	$12,013,000
First National Bank of Chicago	Kevin Reardon	$460,000	7.98	$460,000
Average		$4,970,695	18.08	$7,249,478

In the late 1990s, global banks are joined by a host of other institutions that are fueling the explosion of private financial flows.

PENSION FUNDS: Between 1991 and 1996, the segment of pension funds allocated to overseas stocks rose 30 percent a year to a point where in 1996, 11 percent of the total assets of pension funds were overseas.

MUTUAL FUNDS: Mutual funds have spawned two instruments for overseas investing: global funds which can buy stocks in the United States and overseas, and international funds that invest only overseas. The number of mutual funds that invested all or some of their portfolio overseas jumped from 29 in 1984 to 658 in 1996, with the value of assets in these funds skyrocketing from $5 billion to $264 billion.

FOUNDATIONS AND UNIVERSITIES: Many of these institutions are also diversifying their portfolios to include emerging and other overseas markets. In March 1997, Vanderbilt University in Tennessee shifted about $60 million out of the U.S. stock market into the hands of a team of international money managers to invest overseas, raising the university's endowment allocation in foreign markets to 20 percent of the total.

HOW DO CORPORATIONS EXERCISE THEIR POWER?

Most large corporations and banks maintain their own extensive lobbying operations and donate large sums to political campaigns (see p. 38). In addition, corporations have pooled their resources to promote globalization policies that serve their interests.

The Corporate Coalitions

USA*NAFTA: Corporate America carried out one of the most expansive (and expensive) lobbying efforts in history to win passage of the North American Free Trade Agreement in 1993. The driving force was a business coalition called USA*NAFTA. Calling itself a "grassroots" organization, USA*NAFTA gave new meaning to the term by enlisting thirty-five Fortune 500 companies as "captains" to whip up support for the agreement in each of the fifty U.S. states. An army of more than 2,000 USA*NAFTA member corporations and business associations provided back-up, and contributed mightily to NAFTA's passage. During the months leading up to the vote, USA*NAFTA lobbyists wearing matching red, white, and blue neckties swarmed through Congressional office buildings. Top coalition spokespersons appeared frequently on national television, gave testimony before Congress, and exhibited their export products on the White House lawn.

Other recent examples of corporate coalitions for free trade:

ALLIANCE FOR GATT NOW: Claimed to represent more than 200,000 businesses. Lobbied for the 1994 General Agreement on Tariffs and Trade (GATT) agreement, which established the World Trade Organization. One of the Alliance's more unusual publicity stunts was to produce decks of glossy "trading cards," one for each U.S. state, highlighting the agreement's supposed benefits.

AMERICA LEADS ON TRADE: About 450 corporations and 120 trade associations whose aim was to obtain passage of "fast-track" trade negotiating authority. ALOT aired TV commercials in 104 swing Congressional districts promoting fast-track.

USA*ENGAGE: More than 600 businesses and associations have come together since 1997 to oppose unilateral U.S. trade sanctions, such as those applied to India for nuclear testing and Burma for human rights violations.

The Business Associations

While the corporate coalitions tend to come and go with specific legislative campaigns, the following U.S. associations maintain a strong voice for global firms in the halls of Congress, the media, and the courts. Similar groupings can be found in other nations.

BUSINESS ROUNDTABLE: Club for the CEOs of the Fortune 500. The Roundtable is also the driving force behind many of the campaign-oriented coalitions.

U.S. COUNCIL FOR INTERNATIONAL BUSINESS: Ensures that the interests of global firms are heard by international agencies such as the International Labor Organization, World Trade Organization (WTO), and the Organization for Economic Cooperation and Development.

U.S. CHAMBER OF COMMERCE: The biggest business organization in the world and claims to be the "principal advocate for the American business community." Chamber head Thomas Donahue made a forty-city tour to promote fast-track and claimed to mobilize 50,000 "activists" to call their Congressional representatives.

NATIONAL FOREIGN TRADE COUNCIL: 580 companies involved in trade. Filed suit against the Commonwealth of Massachusetts for its law prohibiting state agencies from purchasing goods or services from companies that do business in Myanmar (formerly Burma), a country known for rampant human rights violations.

The Corporate Think Tanks

The five major Washington-based pro-globalization think tanks had combined budgets in of $87.6 million 1997. Corporate contributions comprise as much as 30 percent of their budgets and top executives figure prominently on their boards.

HERITAGE FOUNDATION: Think tank of the far right. Offered blueprint for the Reagan White House. Produces hundreds of policy reports and briefs for Congress each year.

AMERICAN ENTERPRISE INSTITUTE: Often referred to as the think tank of the Fortune 500. Major backer of free trade deals.

BROOKINGS INSTITUTION: Published *Globaphobia* in 1998, which suggests that public concerns about globalization are rooted in misinformation. Co-author Robert Z. Lawrence holds a new Brookings Chair in International Trade and Economics funded by Toyota Motor Corporation.

CATO INSTITUTE: Libertarian think tank that opposes all government interference in the market. Bashes even the IMF as a market meddler. In addition to a program on "Global Economic Liberty," Cato established a new Center for Trade Policy Studies in 1997.

INSTITUTE FOR INTERNATIONAL ECONOMICS: Promotes free trade initiatives such as NAFTA and WTO, while generally opposing "interventionist" solutions to international trade imbalances. Has received as much as 6 percent of its funding from the Japanese government.

B. PUBLIC INSTITUTIONS

During the Great Depression of the 1930s, stock markets around the world collapsed, factories came to a grinding halt, banks went under, and trade flows collapsed as nations erected protectionist barriers. The architects of the post–World War II global economic institutions wanted, above all else, to set in place barriers against a similar collapse. Because the United States emerged from that war with as much as half the globe's measured industrial production and four-fifths of its gold reserves, U.S. negotiators were well-positioned to ensure that the rules favored continued U.S. dominance.[10]

The vision was to create public international institutions to anchor each of the three pillars of global economic activity:

- production: World Bank
- finance: International Monetary Fund
- trade: GATT, succeeded in 1995 by the WTO

British and American negotiators at a conference in Bretton Woods, New Hampshire, created the World Bank to help with reconstruction after the war and to assist long-term production in poorer countries, and the International Monetary Fund (IMF) to oversee the international financial and monetary order. The institution to free restrictions on trade, the GATT, was set up last and was replaced in 1995 by a more powerful WTO. Other public institutions have been created since World War II to supplement the activities of each of the original three, but none match the power and breadth of the World Bank, the IMF, and now the WTO.

We offer a snapshot of the three and some of their progeny, and of the moves by global corporations to twist the public institutions to serve their narrow interests.

Production: The World Bank

By far the largest of the public global economic institutions, the World Bank employs over 11,000 people, has offices in 65 of its 181 member nations, and routinely lends more than $20 billion a year.

Unlike other UN agencies, the World Bank—like the regional development banks and the IMF—does not operate on a "one nation, one vote" system. Instead, governance is closer to the "he who pays the piper, picks the tune" model. Countries have voting power pegged to the size of their economies (and their financial contribution to the Bank). Accordingly, the United States and other rich nations dominate. During the Cold War, the United States frequently used the World Bank (and the IMF) as an arm of U.S. foreign policy to aid allies and punish enemies.

Most of the World Bank's lending goes to fund "development" projects: long-term, low interest loans to build dams, power plants, and fund agricultural "modernization." Noble as this may sound, the Bank's Articles of Agreements state as a principle goal "to promote foreign private investments." Indeed, the U.S. Treasury Department promotes U.S. government funding of the World Bank as a way to boost U.S. firms. A top Treasury Department official bragged to Congress in 1995 that for every dollar the U.S. contributes to the World Bank, U.S. corporations receive $1.30 in procurement contracts.[11]

Hence, what might have become a development institution has largely evolved into a facilitator of global corporations' overseas investments, often with devastating consequences for the environment, communities, and workers. None have benefited more than agribusiness firms and energy firms; more than two-fifths of World Bank loans during its over half-century existence have gone to these two sectors. For decades, the World Bank has been the world's largest promoter of chemical-intensive agriculture. Agrochemical firms from the United States and Europe have been the prime beneficiaries.

ENERGY BONANZA

Institute for Policy Studies researcher Daphne Wysham has calculated that nine out of ten energy-related projects financed by the World Bank benefit at least one corporation headquartered in the United States or one of the other six main industrial powers. At the same time, World Bank projects have become major contributors to greenhouse gas emissions. Wysham also found that World Bank oil, gas, and coal projects initiated between 1992 and 1998 would add an amount of carbon to earth's atmosphere equivalent to one and a half times that emitted by all the world's countries in one year. These energy projects invariably provide electricity to export-oriented firms and seldom meet the growing energy needs of the world's poorest, two billion of whom live without access to electricity. Many of the corporations that benefit from World Bank contracts comprise the misleadingly labeled Global Climate Coalition, a network of industries that lobby to prevent the U.S. from taking action on climate change.

Source: *The World Bank: A Tale of Power, Plunder, and Resistance* by Alec Dubro and Mike Konopacki, published by Public Services International.

FOR FIVE YEARS WE HAVE BEEN FIGHTING THE DESTRUCTION OF OUR FAMILIES, OUR LIVELIHOODS, OUR ENVIRONMENT!

STRUCTURAL ADJUSTMENT

In 1980, the World Bank added a new component to its operations. Beyond project lending, it began offering large "balance of payments" loans to governments in return for "structural" changes in policy. The Bank claimed that many countries were holding themselves back by restricting trade and investment. The new mantra of the 1980s (popularized by the Reagan, Thatcher, and Kohl governments as well as the World Bank) was free markets: free up trade and investment and the market will offer growth and prosperity.

The debt crisis, which peaked in 1982, gave the World Bank the leverage to force countries to accept the free market mantra. In return for new loans, debt-ridden countries agreed to carry out "Structural Adjustment Programs" (SAPs) of the World Bank or similar conditions attached to IMF facilities. We detail these conditions in the next section on the IMF.

Finance: The International Monetary Fund and the MAI

The IMF delegation fled at dawn. As the Indonesian capital still smoldered from the May 14 fires set by rioters during Jakarta's most devastating demonstrations yet, eight expatriates working for the International Monetary Fund and two spouses set out for the military airport to catch a chartered flight out of the country. Leaving early to avoid bandits searching cars along the way, they skirted burned-out trucks, toppled lampposts, and debris. In a final humiliation, immigration officials kept the group at the airport—first finding fault with their visas, then using them to bargain for a planeload of food and water. After six hours and phone calls to government officials, the IMF staff finally boarded an evacuation plane to Singapore.

—"Up in Smoke," *Business Week*, June 1, 1998.

Why such anger in May 1998 by Indonesians toward the International Monetary Fund? After all, the IMF was set up in 1944 to help calm financial problems around the world. In its early years, the IMF performed two important functions. First, if the price of cotton plummeted and Tanzania faced a short-term balance of payments crisis through no fault of its own, the IMF could rush in with short-term financing. Second, from World War II to 1971, all currencies were fixed to the U.S. dollar; the IMF helped with loans when currencies were under pressure. When the Nixon administration ended fixed exchange rates, the IMF searched for a new mission.

During the 1980s, the IMF's role shifted in two ways:

1.   It focused more on ensuring that private investors and banks were shielded from large losses when their developing-country investments went bad, rather than helping governments avoid currency crises.

2.   The IMF began imposing much more stringent conditions on countries that received its loans. In the 1960s and 1970s, transnational banks had loaned hundreds of billions of dollars to poorer nations, often for giant ecologically damaging projects such as dams, or five-star hotels, or nuclear power plants. Much of the money lined the pockets of corrupt dictators or entrepreneurs, and by the early 1980s much of it could not be repaid. In August 1982, Mexico was the first large debtor to announce that it could not service its debts and the IMF was again brought center stage. In a series of deals with different countries, the U.S. Treasury Department and the large banks told countries that they would get no new loans (to repay the old ones) until they agreed to an IMF package. Now the world's financial policeman, the IMF pressed for a series of measures that steered scarce resources in poorer countries toward repaying creditors in the richer countries.

A typical World Bank/IMF adjustment package includes the following:

WORLD BANK/IMF CONDITIONS

POLICY	IMPACT
cut government spending	• less money for education, health care, and environment
devalue currency and export more	• accelerates plunder of natural resources for export, increases global pressures to compete by cutting prices and wages
liberalize financial markets	• more volatile short-term investment
reduce real wages and cut government price subsidies	• workers suffer and prices on rice, cooking oil, and other necessities skyrocket, often leading to riots
increase interest rates to attract foreign capital	• domestic business bankruptcies, crisis for individuals with debts

Most developing countries—particularly in Latin America and Africa, and increasingly in the transition countries of east and central Europe—have implemented or are in the process of implementing IMF agreements or World Bank SAPs.

Source: *A Journey Through the Global Debt Crisis*, a production of the Debt Crisis Network, 1988.

While often succeeding in shrinking government budget deficits, eliminating hyperinflation, and maintaining debt-payment schedules, S A P s have exposed developing countries to the worst aspects of the global economy. Their impact on people, particularly women, children, and the poor, has been devastating.[12]

- In Senegal, touted by the IMF as a success story because of increased growth rates, unemployment increased from 25 percent in 1991 to 44 percent in 1996.

- Zimbabwe's SAP forced the reintroduction of school fees, leading to drops in attendance, especially for girls, while a one-third cut in health spending is linked to a doubling of deaths of women during childbirth.

- Costa Rica, the first Central American country to implement a SAP, saw real wages decline by 16.9 percent between 1980 and 1991. A 35 percent cut in health programs led to a dramatic increase in infectious disease rates and infant mortality.

- During the first four years of Hungary's SAP, unemployment rose from 0 percent to 13 percent. Between 1989 and 1996, the value of wages fell by 24 percent.

THE FINANCIAL CASINO

In the go-go stock market boom of the 1990s, the IMF linked up with the U.S. Treasury Department to insist that more "protectionist" nations of Asia eliminate restrictions on the inflow of foreign capital. The result was an explosion of private money into Asia and the big Latin American economies (see chart on p.19). While such flows make millionaires on Wall Street and in the financial districts of Bangkok, Mexico City, and Jakarta, they also can devastate economies when economic conditions deteriorate and investors get scared. In December 1994 in Mexico and in July 1997 in Asia, investors got spooked and billions of dollars flowed out overnight. Currencies plunged, stock markets crashed, and millions of people fell into poverty in a financial crisis with long-term effects all over the world.

There is an ongoing debate among both policy elites and academics as to the desirability of unregulated capital markets, especially for developing countries. Washington University professor David Felix has pointed out that this drive to liberalize financial markets is in direct violation of the IMF's Articles of Agreement, which authorize IMF member nations "to exercise such controls as are necessary to regulate international capital movements."[13]

The Multilateral Agreement on Investment

Global banks and corporations began clamoring in the mid-1990s for a new agreement to further pressure nations to remove controls on investment. The result is a proposed treaty called the Multilateral Agreement on Investment (MAI). The MAI would limit governments' ability to regulate foreign investment, thus enhancing both the mobility and the bargaining power of multinational corporations. Canadian citizen leader Maude Barlow has called the MAI "a corporate bill of rights." The proposal first surfaced in the World Trade Organization in 1996. When several developing nations expressed reservations about the proposed agreement, negotiators shifted the venue to the rich nations club: the Organization of Economic Cooperation and Development (OECD) in Paris, where governments of twenty-nine of the world's richest nations meet to discuss policy. By late 1998, the OECD had failed to reach an agreement because of stiff citizen protests in at least a dozen of the twenty-nine OECD nations. Since then, negotiators have shifted strategy and are attempting to slip parts of the MAI into the WTO or the IMF.

COMPONENTS OF THE DRAFT MAI:

1. Prohibit local, state, and federal governments from giving preference to local or domestic companies when awarding contracts.

2. Prohibit governments from requiring a certain level of domestic-made content in purchases.

3. Prohibit governments from requiring a company to invest a certain amount or employ a certain number of people when establishing an operation on its territory.

4. Eliminate governments' restrictions on foreign ownership of various industries.

5. Prohibit a government from seizing assets without immediate and full compensation.

6. Discourage the use of investment incentives, such as tax breaks and job training programs, to lure corporations.

7. Do away with limits on capital movements.

8. Allow corporations to sue governments over laws that they believe violate the treaty. International dispute panels would rule on these cases and could impose monetary damages.

"To succeed in today's world markets . . . a company can't hope to sit back home in Dubuque making widgets and then export the finished goods to buyers abroad. . . . To gain a foothold in an overseas market, you need to invest."

—Lawrence A. Bossidy, chairman and CEO, AlliedSignal, quoted in U.S. Council for International Business, "A Guide to the MAI," November 1996

The Alphabet Soup of Free Trade:
GATT, the WTO, and NAFTA

Over fifty years ago, as the world began to rebuild from the ashes of World War II, a healthy and broad-based discussion emerged over the shape of a new global institution to govern trade. Government negotiators worked on the framework of a new institution to be called the International Trade Organization. The institution was designed to balance the economic goal of liberalizing global trade with the social goal of stimulating full employment. It also set the principle that poorer nations deserved special treatment in trade in order to close the gap between rich and poor nations.

The U.S. Senate did not, however, share the same framework. It rejected the broad mandate of the proposed International Trade Organization and instead the world's leading nations approved a much smaller organization called the General Agreement on Tariffs and Trade. The GATT contained mechanisms to reduce barriers to trade in goods and services. It contained no measures to press for full employment or to encourage development proactively. Rather, it enshrined the concept that all countries must treat goods from all other countries on equal grounds.

TOBACCO FREE TRADE

Just as transnational banks and corporations came to twist World Bank and IMF operations toward their narrow ends, so too did they deploy the GATT to break open new markets. U.S. tobacco giants have faced a major marketing challenge as health campaigns slow the growth of cigarette sales in the United States and Western Europe. With their future tied to spreading cigarette sales in the poorer countries of the world, the companies have faced barriers in a number of nations, particularly in Asia, where governments placed restrictions on imports. Starting in the 1980s, tobacco companies went to work. With major tobacco company contributions paving the way, the U.S. government began threatening the governments of Japan, Taiwan, South Korea, Thailand, and China to open their cigarette markets or face the prospect of some combination of U.S. bilateral sanctions and U.S. charges of discriminatory behavior under the GATT. A GATT tribunal ruled that Thailand must open its market, and one by one the pressures have yielded new markets to the tobacco transnationals. Only the bonanza of the China market remains unconquered and the U.S. government has demanded that China open its cigarette markets if it wants to join the successor to the GATT, the WTO.

THE WORLD TRADE ORGANIZATION

Starting in the mid-1980s, the U.S. government began sketching the plans to replace the GATT with a larger organization equipped with more powerful tools to break down barriers to trade and investment. Negotiations were completed in 1994, and the WTO replaced the GATT in 1995. Unlike the GATT, whose powers centered on reducing tariff barriers, the WTO machinery can be deployed to eliminate any perceived barrier to trade and investment. These can include health, safety, or environmental laws which other nations believe are unfair barriers to trade. Developing countries were particularly concerned that transnational corporations would use the WTO as a battering ram to knock down the last barriers they had to foreign investment. Nevertheless, as Mauritius's representative stated after completion of the blueprint for the WTO, "We lost everything, but we will put our head on the block with dignity."

WTO AND DEMOCRACY

WTO negotiations and dispute hearings take place behind closed doors in Geneva, Switzerland. Although U.S. negotiators must consult with nongovernmental advisory committees, these entities are dominated by corporate lobbyists, while labor unions and environmental groups have only a few seats. So-called trade experts, picked from a set roster by government representatives, hold the power to rule on WTO disputes. Public Citizen points out one indication of the lack of diversity on the roster of experts—92.5 percent are men.

BANANA SPLIT

The WTO has handled more than 125 disputes among its member countries. Rulings are binding, so losing governments must fix the offending trade regulation or provide compensation. Refusal may lead to trade sanctions, as in the case of the "Banana Wars" between the United States and the European Union (EU). This dispute arose over an EU policy of giving preferential treatment to bananas grown in its former colonies in the Caribbean and Africa. The United States complained that the policy was unfair to banana-producing Latin American nations and the WTO agreed. When the EU refused to change the policy, the United States threatened in October 1998 to place 100 percent tariffs on some EU imports, essentially doubling their price for American consumers. Bananas are a curious focus for a U.S. trade war, because not a single banana is grown in the continental United States. U.S. officials claim that the battle is over the principles of "fair trade." However, there are strong suspicions that the U.S. position was simply purchased by Chiquita, a U.S.-based firm with the most to lose from the EU policy because of its extensive banana plantations in Latin America. According to the Center for Responsive Politics, Chiquita's CEO Carl Lindner and his family, his companies, and their executives gave $5 million to political candidates and parties between 1991 and 1998.[14]

Cartoon in a Canadian publication: Canada and many other countries view competition between the multi-billion dollar U.S. cultural industry and their own as slightly lopsided.

THE NORTH AMERICAN FREE TRADE AGREEMENT

At the beginning of the 1990s, the U.S. government proposed accelerating the free trade agenda by negotiating regional free trade and investment deals. The first proposal was to create a massive unified North American market by establishing a North American Free Trade Agreement (NAFTA). NAFTA set out to do three things:

1. eliminate barriers to trade between Mexico, the United States, and Canada over fifteen years;
2. eliminate barriers to investment;
3. provide new protections for global corporations against piracy of CDs, videos, and other "intellectual property."

In addition, after unions and environmental groups raised strong objections to NAFTA, the three governments negotiated NAFTA "side agreements" to deal with concerns over the impact of free trade on labor and the environment. The labor agreement established agencies called National Administrative Offices (NAOs) in each of the three countries to deal with complaints regarding violations of domestic labor laws. The environmental agreement set up a similar agency and also created a North American Development Bank (NADBank) designed to provide low-interest loans for environmental infrastructure projects on the U.S.-Mexico border.

The battle over NAFTA's passage was a bloody one, with a broad coalition of labor, environmental, family farm, and other nongovernment groups united against the pact's formidable supporters, including the Fortune 500 companies and the Clinton administration. Congress passed the agreement by a margin of thirty-four votes in November 1993 and it went into effect January 1, 1994.

THE NAFTA CONTROVERSY RAGES ON

NAFTA MATH

Much of the skepticism about NAFTA stems from a broad public understanding that many of the promises made by the agreement's supporters were overblown or simply false. For example, the Clinton administration sold NAFTA primarily as a jobs program. The argument was that the lifting of trade barriers with our neighbors would result in an improvement in the U.S. trade balance, that is that our exports to Canada and Mexico would expand faster than our imports. These exports would then support a net increase in U.S. jobs. When the prediction proved false and the U.S. trade balance with Canada and Mexico worsened, the administration revised its formula and applied what the *Wall Street Journal* refers to as "NAFTAMath." Suddenly, it was only the export side of the equation that was significant, even though increased imports clearly have a negative impact on U.S. jobs.

LABOR AND ENVIRONMENTAL CONCERNS

Although NAFTA's side agreements represent a step forward in establishing the link between trade and labor and environment, the concrete benefits of these pacts have been disappointing. Unions and other groups have filed more than ten complaints of labor violations, but even when the NAO has confirmed the charges, the outcomes have not directly helped the workers. For example, in a case against Sony, the NAO found that the company had denied its workers in Nuevo Laredo the right to organize, and that the Mexican government had "persistently failed to enforce its own laws" in the area. Nonetheless, no concrete remedies or financial sanctions have been imposed, and the company and the government have failed to change their behavior.

The environmental pact has been even more discouraging. The NADBank was supposed to provide low-interest loans totalling up to $3 billion for environmental projects. As of mid-1998, not a single environmental project financed by the NADBank was in operation. Meanwhile, about 1,000 new maquiladoras opened during this period, further straining environmental infrastructure in the border region.[15]

NAFTA's Vicious Cycle

1. INCREASED U.S. CORN EXPORTS: During NAFTA's first three years, U.S. corn exports to Mexico increased an astounding 1,267 percent, from $75 million to $1 billion.[16] On the surface, this sounds like good news for U.S. farmers and for Mexicans looking for lower prices on their staple food. The reality is more complicated.

7. U.S. AGRIBUSINESS: By contrast, the revenues of corporate grain traders Cargill and Continental Grain increased 20 and 7 percent, respectively, in NAFTA's first three years.[18] These firms helped pressure Mexico to allow duty-free U.S. corn imports.

6. U.S. FARMERS: Congress justified cuts in agricultural subsidies by claiming that increased exports would in part make up the difference. Instead, U.S. farmers, at the mercy of volatile international markets and weather, are facing their worst crisis since the 1980s. Family farmers are expected to drop to less than one percent of the total population—close to extinction.

Congressional passage of NAFTA in 1993 and the WTO in 1994 emboldened the administration to embark on a frenzy of new negotiations for regional free trade deals. These include:

- proposed expansion of NAFTA benefits to the Caribbean and Central American countries;
- creation of a Free Trade area of the Americas by 2005;
- creation of an Asia free trade area under the auspices of the Asia-Pacific Economic Cooperation (APEC) discussions;
- creation of a free trade agreement with Africa.

2. FARMERS UPROOTED: Hundreds of thousands of Mexican peasants, unable to compete with U.S. producers, have been driven from their land. Once able to feed their own families, they must now obtain cash to buy food, despite limited income opportunities.

5. U.S. BORDER: U.S. spending on immigration controls has skyrocketed (see p. 34) and an anti-immigrant backlash has created tensions throughout the country.

4. IMMIGRATION PRESSURES: Uprooted Mexican farmers have contributed to increased immigration flows to the United States. According to the Institute for Agriculture and Trade Policy, "in one of free trade's brutal ironies, many of these Mexican trade policy refugees are joining the swelling flow of immigrants who are harvesting and processing U.S. food in often dangerous and low-wage conditions."

3. POVERTY INCREASE: The United Nations reports that two-thirds of Mexicans were living in poverty in 1999, up from less than half in 1994.[17]

v. Responses to Globalization

There is no denying that the promoters of corporate-driven globalization are
a formidable force. The bulk of this book has been devoted to illustrating the nature
of their economic and political clout and examining the arguments that they
offer in their defense. But we also want to emphasize that there is nothing inevitable
about the current direction of globalization. Yes, corporations have used their
tremendous power to shape many of the rules of the road for globalization
to meet their own narrow interests. In the 1990s, they have escalated their efforts
with sweeping new rules at the local, national, and global levels
to enhance their mobility across borders.

And yet in the United States and elsewhere, this decade has also been
one of growing resistance to global corporations. Millions of workers,
consumers, environmentalists, religious activists, farmers, and women around
the world are demanding their fair share of the fruits of the global
economy. Their strategies are diverse. Some attempt to stop
or slow down aspects of globalization, while others aim to reshape
its path in ways that promote democracy, equity, and
sustainability. Campaigns operate on the local, national,
and international levels. Some are high-profile
and media-driven, while others, in the face of extreme
oppression, operate off camera.

Leaders Recognize the Social Impacts of Globalization

KOFI ANNAN, UN secretary-general, speaking at Harvard University, September 17, 1998:

Throughout much of the developing world, globalization is seen, not as a term describing objective reality, but as an ideology of predatory capitalism. Whatever reality there is in this view, the perception of a siege is unmistakable. Millions of people are suffering; savings have been decimated; decades of hard-won progress in the fight against poverty are imperiled. And unless the basic principles of equity and liberty are defended in the political arena and advanced as critical conditions for economic growth, they may suffer rejection. Economic despair will be followed by political turmoil and many of the advances for freedom of the last half-century could be lost.

POPE JOHN PAUL II, Mexico City, January 23, 1999:

There is an economic globalization which brings some positive consequences.... However, if globalization is ruled merely by the laws of the market applied to suit the powerful, the consequences cannot but be negative. These are, for example, the absolutizing of the economy, unemployment, the reduction and deterioration of public services, the destruction of the environment and natural resources, the growing distance between rich and poor, and unfair competition which puts the poor nations in a situation of ever-increasing inferiority.

SUBCOMANDANTE MARCOS, communique following the January 1, 1994, uprising of the Zapatistas in southern Mexico:

NAFTA is a death sentence for indigenous people.

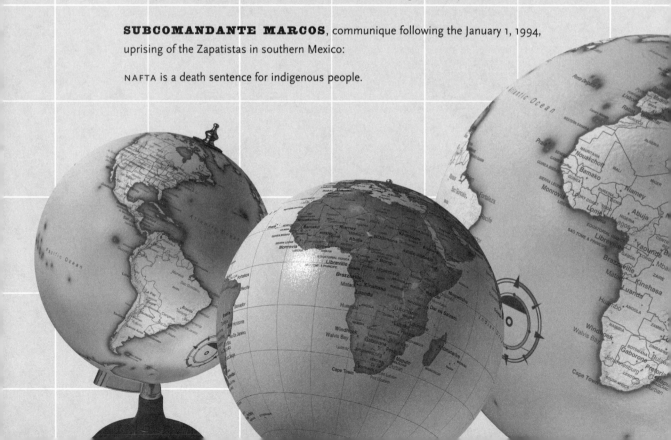

NELSON MANDELA, President of South Africa, Conference to mark the fiftieth anniversary of the GATT, Geneva, Switzerland, May 1998:

Though international trade and investment have always been an integral part of the world economy, the extent to which all parties have benefited has depended on the circumstances in which they have taken place. The current process of globalization is no exception.... Fifty years ago, [when the GATT was founded] few would have imagined that the exploitation of the world's abundant resources and a prodigious growth in world trade would have seen the gap between rich and poor widening.

AUN SAN SUU KYI, Nobel Peace Prize recipient and pro-democracy leader in Myanmar, Rangoon, September 1996:

Until we have a system that guarantees rule of law and basic democratic institutions, no amount of aid or investment will benefit our people. Profits from business enterprises will merely go towards enriching a small, already very privileged elite.

SUSAN GEORGE, Associate Director, Transnational Institute, January 1999 issue of *Le Monde Diplomatique*:

Had they designed a commercial or residential high-rise, the architects of the international financial system would have been dragged into court for criminal negligence and fraud. Whole sections of their edifice are crashing down, and, as typically happens in such circumstances, the falling masonry crushes innocent victims whose only mistake is to be in the wrong place at the wrong time.

A. PROTESTING THE RULES OF GLOBALIZATION

Many citizens efforts have begun to challenge the dominant approach to globalization. In recent years, three fights in particular have rattled the foundation of the globalization giants.

Fast-Track Attack

In the fall of 1997, the most powerful U.S. corporations joined with the U.S. President and the leadership of the U.S. Congress to promote legislation that would enable the government to negotiate more free trade and investment liberalization deals. (This power, called fast-track authority, allows the President to negotiate trade pacts and send them to Congress for a vote without amendment.) Hundreds of labor, environmental, farm, "development," and other groups opposed the legislation. The new, dynamic leadership of the AFL-CIO mobilized its forces, while a number of environmental and Latino groups that had supported NAFTA shifted to opposition because of NAFTA's failure to clean up the U.S.–Mexico border or come through with community loans supporters had promised. After months of battle, President Clinton admitted defeat on November 10. It was an important turning point in the debate over the rules of globalization.

The fast-track effort built on the early 1990s battles over the World Trade Organization and the North American Free Trade Agreement, which brought together groups representing many countries and sectors of society. The anti–WTO coalitions, initiated by the Institute for Agriculture and Trade Policy, the Third World Network, and dozens of other groups, created a global movement to oppose the creation of a more powerful, less accountable global trade body. The anti–NAFTA coalitions were historic in that they wrenched international economic policy out of the hands of a few in government and business and, for the first time, created a broad public debate involving thousands of workers, environmentalists, family farmers, consumer advocates and other activists. Although the pro–NAFTA forces ultimately prevailed, the opposition learned a great deal from this experience, paving the way for the defeat of fast-track and permanently broadening the national debate on the global economy.

The fast-track battle also benefited from work initiated during the NAFTA debate to articulate an alternative vision for the global economy. Thanks to years of dialogue among North American scholars and activists, a considerable number of fast-track opponents could offer a viable alternative to the NAFTA model that protected the rights and interests of workers, communities, and the environment. Activists continue to broaden and deepen their proposals for alternatives to free trade. For example, in the fall of 1998, citizens coalitions from four countries (including the U.S.-based Alliance for Responsible Trade) released a detailed alternative to the Free Trade Area of the Americas.

THE ALTERNATIVE VISION IS SPREADING[1]
Percentage of Americans who believe trade agreements should advance:
environmental protections 87%   labor protections 73%

Multilateral Agreement on Investment
In the fall of 1998, the pro-globalization side suffered another setback. In the face of widespread international opposition, the member governments of the Organization for Economic Cooperation and Development (OECD) suspended negotiations for a Multilateral Agreement on Investment. The MAI would reduce the power of the twenty-nine OECD member countries and any additional signatory countries to place restrictions on foreign investment. The Malaysia-based Third World Network first alerted activists around the world to the MAI proposals in 1996. The dynamic Council of Canadians picked up the call and spread protests across Canada. These groups, along with the International Forum on Globalization, helped galvanize resistance campaigns in France, the United States, and eight other countries to promote public scrutiny about what the negotiators were doing behind closed doors. In the United States, Public Citizen posted a leaked draft of the deal on the Internet and worked with Friends of the Earth, the Preamble Center, and other groups to coordinate an intense exchange of information through email. According to the Canadian *Globe and Mail*, the high-powered OECD politicians were "no match for a global band of grassroots organizations, which, with little more than computers and access to the Internet, helped derail the deal."[2]

IMF and the Global Financial Casino

Since the early 1980s, demonstrators have gathered in Mexico City, Manila, Caracas, and other cities to protest what they view as harsh IMF conditions. Protesters have parodied the IMF's initials as everything from the "Imelda Marcos Foundation" to "I M Fired." The protests escalated around the world in 1997 and 1998 as the economies of Thailand, Indonesia, South Korea, and Russia sank into depression in the wake of IMF-mandated policy reforms. Even large segments of the business community in these countries came out against the IMF. In the United States, opposition to IMF conditions grew as cash-starved Asian nations cut imports of U.S. products and as the U.S. stock market began to swing wildly in response to economic gyrations of foreign currencies and stock markets. Throughout 1998 Congress stalled on granting new funds to the IMF as progressives decried IMF austerity and free market Republicans accused the IMF of bailing out imprudent bank lenders. When Congress finally approved the funds in late 1998, they conditioned them on reforms within the IMF. By September 1998, citizen groups around the world were converging on an agenda to reorient financial systems to serve the credit needs of communities and a healthy environment (see Appendix 1).

The battles over fast-track, MAI, and the IMF revealed the heightened understanding among the general public that free trade and investment liberalization have increased corporate power to bargain down wages, working conditions, and health and environmental standards everywhere. This is not to say that the pro-globalization forces have given up. As we write this, they are mounting a renewed war to influence public opinion and win back fast-track authority. MAI negotiations are said to be continuing "underground," and the IMF controversy rages on.

Nevertheless, these fights have given renewed hope to activists around the world who are working to combat the negative impacts of globalization. Each of the three fights has strengthened cross-border cooperation within specific sectors, such as labor and environmental movements. Each has also stimulated new cross-border organizing and education efforts that span several sectors. New groups such as the San Francisco-based International Forum on Globalization are providing an initial infrastructure for continuing cross-border dialogue, education, and strategizing.

In this section we have tried to organize the multitude of efforts by showing how people are using their power as workers, shareholders, consumers, students, voters, and artists. Many of these strategies overlap and choosing just a few specific campaigns to highlight was difficult—signs of the richness of this movement.

B. WORKER POWER

Cross-border union solidarity has deep roots, leading back into the early decades of this century. In the late 1990s, a reinvigorated U.S. labor movement has increased its efforts in international solidarity work. One highlight was the AFL-CIO's successful campaign in 1997–98 to obtain the release of Indonesian labor leader Muchtar Pakpahan, who had been jailed under the repressive Suharto regime. Working with other labor and human rights groups, the AFL-CIO persuaded the U.S. government to threaten to cut off Indonesia's trade benefits and apply other economic pressures unless Pakpahan was released. By early 1999, Pakpahan had already succeeded in gaining recognition for about 80 democratic unions. In addition to the AFL-CIO, a number of U.S. unions, often linked to local labor/community coalitions and other independent groups, are at the forefront of efforts to use worker power to combat the negative impacts of globalization. Here are a few lessons from their experiences:

1. Corporate Globalization Requires Union Organizing Across Borders

Even the most powerful U.S. unions are learning that they cannot fight transnational corporate giants alone. A prime example is the successful resolution of the 1997 Teamsters strike against the United Parcel Service (UPS), which focused on the corporate strategy of shifting from full-time to part-time and temporary jobs with lower pay and fewer benefits.

This leaflet was translated into five languages to explain the UPS strike in the United States to European supporters.

Although UPS dominates the U.S. market for small-package delivery, the firm is more vulnerable in Europe, where it faces stiff competition from a number of other companies. UPS workers in England, Belgium, Germany, the Netherlands, and France supported the U.S. workers by carrying out sympathy strikes, leafleting, and other solidarity actions. According to then-Teamster International

Representative Andy Banks, "enlightened self-interest was the key. European UPS workers and their unions reasoned that if the 185,000 striking Teamsters could not stop the part-time, subcontracting mentality of the company, what could a few hundred or a few thousand workers hope to achieve in the smaller UPS European operations?" Banks points out that unions also worked to block UPS deliveries in India, the Philippines, and Spain during the strike.[3]

2. Solidarity Is a Two-Way Street

In some countries, U.S. unions are providing direct support for organizing campaigns. In the Dominican Republic, for example, the U.S.-based UNITE apparel union and the AFL-CIO have helped local activists obtain seven union contracts at plants in the country's export processing zone. As U.S. unions become more sophisticated in their international work, they are also finding that they have much to learn from their fellow unionists in the developing world.

The U.S.-based United Electrical Workers union (UE) and the Mexico-based Frente Auténtico del Trabajo (FAT) began a formal alliance in 1992 that UE organizers say has benefited their union as much as their Mexican counterparts. In 1995, the UE and FAT worked together on an organizing drive at Milwaukee-based Aluminum Casting and Engineering, a large employer of recent Mexican immigrants who had come north to escape poverty. Instead, the Mexican-born workers found low wages and hazardous working conditions not unlike those in Mexico. But fear of retaliation by plant officials and cultural and language barriers discouraged these workers from joining UE's union effort. Some U.S.-born workers, frustrated by their inability to demand higher wages, scapegoated their immigrant coworkers. Stymied by these problems, the UE enlisted the help of Roberto Valerio, one of the leaders of a FAT affiliate. Valerio was able to dispel cultural misunderstandings and embolden the Mexican rank and file to vote in the union. (The National Labor Relations Board later overturned the union victory on a technicality.)

Mexican unions have also supported U.S. workers by filing complaints on their behalf under NAFTA. The NAFTA labor agreement established agencies in each country to handle charges regarding a government's failure to enforce labor rights. Although the majority of cases have been filed by U.S. groups alleging violations in Mexico, Mexican groups have filed two cases on behalf of U.S. workers. The first targeted a Sprint subsidiary in California with a primarily Latino workforce. The case helped draw attention to the corporate tactic of busting unions by closing plants that are the sites of organizing drives. The case also provided a platform for an international campaign targeting Sprint among U.S., Mexican, and European telephone workers unions. The second case, filed by a coalition of Mexican unions and farmworker groups, charges the U.S. government with failing to protect the rights of Washington state apple workers. At press time, this case remained under review.

3. Broader Social Movement for Economic Justice

In their battles with the globalization giants, labor unions are increasingly expanding their power by joining with others in a broader social movement. Some of the most exciting cross-border worker support is being led by organizations that include some unionists but also draw strength from religious, environmental, human rights, and other activists.

COALITION FOR JUSTICE IN THE MAQUILADORAS: CJM is a trinational organization that serves as a bridge between workers, researchers, and activists in all three NAFTA countries. Since its founding in 1989, CJM has supported numerous labor and environmental struggles, coordinated border tours, and conducted dozens of health and safety trainings for Mexican workers. Currently, the CJM is led by the dynamic Martha Ojeda, who worked in the maquiladoras for twenty years.

CJM is made up of more than 100 member organizations, many of which have made tremendous advances in cross-border solidarity over the past few years. One of the best known is the **SUPPORT COMMITTEE FOR MAQUILA- DORA WORKERS**, based in San Diego, which has coordinated international solidarity for a number of labor struggles in Tijuana, Mexico. Their most high-profile effort is an ongoing campaign in support of workers at a factory called Han Young, which produces parts for Hyundai trucks. Although the workers have voted twice to be represented by an independent union, the company has refused to negotiate a contract. Support from some 700 organizations in the United States and Canada helped the workers endure a prolonged strike during the summer of 1998. As this book goes to press, the Han Young fight continues. However, the battle reflects the dramatic change in cross-border solidarity work in the past several years. As SCMW Executive Director Mary Tong explains, "During the NAFTA fight we organized tours for many U.S. unions and other groups but their purpose was mainly just to see what conditions were like for Mexican workers. Now some of those same groups call me and say, 'help us figure out how to do serious solidarity work.'"

Some CJM member groups located far from the border have also made great strides in helping U.S. citizens understand the links between what's happening in their own communities with the global economy:

CROSS-BORDER NETWORK FOR JUSTICE AND SOLIDARITY:
From Kansas City, Missouri, this group has established a sister-community relationship with Nuevo Laredo, Mexico. This city is directly south of Kansas City on I-35, also known as the "NAFTA Superhighway." In the fall of 1997, CBN sent a delegation of labor and social justice activists on a work and study tour that included building a school in cooperation with a maquiladora workers community.

THE TENNESSEE INDUSTRIAL RENEWAL NETWORK: TIRN has coordinated a number of exchanges between U.S. and Mexican workers, in some cases between workers employed by the same corporation. According to TIRN activist Susan Williams, these exchanges have helped Tennesseeans "identify the common culprit"—that it is the corporations that are to blame for job loss in their communities, not Mexican workers.

MINNESOTA FAIR TRADE COALITION: A network of seventy-five labor, environmental, and social justice groups organized primarily to oppose NAFTA and fast-track. It mobilizes support for struggles of maquiladora workers highlighted by CJM. The Fair Trade Coalition is coordinated by the Resource Center of the Americas, which has also developed a Minnesota Clean Clothes Campaign that mobilizes high school students to press for living wages and fair treatment for workers in the global garment industry.

4. Public Humiliation is a Powerful Weapon

In our status-conscious world, many companies are vulnerable to attacks that tarnish their public reputations. One of the most skillful humiliators is the National Labor Committee (NLC) based in New York City, which along with San Francisco-based Global Exchange has worked with a broad array of citizens groups to organize high-profile campaigns against corporate abusers of labor rights. NLC director Charles Kernaghan is known as the man who made TV show host Kathie Lee Gifford cry when he revealed that some of the clothing sold under her name at Wal-Mart was made by children in Central America.

One of the NLC's most successful campaigns focused on the GAP clothing company. Workers who sewed clothing for the GAP at Mandarin International, a contractor based in El Salvador, complained of child labor, forced overtime, unsafe working conditions, and union busting. The NLC organized an intense six-month campaign involving religious, consumer, and other groups in the United States that received tremendous media coverage.

From the NLC's campaign to expose poor treatment of Haitian workers.

In response, the GAP agreed to the demand that Mandarin rehire hundreds of workers fired for organizing activities and to allow human rights organizations to monitor conditions in all Central American factories from which GAP sources. Although the independent union is still fighting for representation, Kernaghan reports that the monitoring has resulted in some concrete improvements, such as air ventilation, clean drinking water, and the elimination of sexual harassment.

Another group that has successfully used the embarrassment weapon is the US/Guatemala Labor Education Project. For several years, US/GLEP coordinated U.S. support for a union organizing drive at a Phillips Van Heusen (PVH) shirt factory in Guatemala. The group used a number of tactics to pressure PVH, but a real breakthrough came when they threatened to protest outside a fundraiser for Human Rights Watch because of the PVH CEO's position on their board. The potential embarrassment prompted a Human Rights Watch investigation of the PVH plant in Guatemala that drove PVH to the bargaining table.[4]

C. SHAREHOLDER POWER

A growing social/ethical investment movement is mobilizing the power of large institutional shareholders to exercise influence over the corporate world. A leader of this movement for a quarter century is the Interfaith Center for Corporate Responsibility, an association of nearly 250 religious denominations. In one recent year, ICCR members submitted 198 shareholder resolutions to press for corporate accountability in the areas of the environment, treatment of workers, and other subjects. Such resolutions seldom pass; however, they serve an important educational function and often lead to further dialogue between the investors and the corporation.

For example, in 1995, the Benedictine Sisters of San Antonio, Texas, filed a shareholder resolution with Alcoa, requesting that the company pay its Mexican workers adequate wages. The resolution never even came up for a vote, but with support from ICCR and the Coalition for Justice in the Maquiladoras, two Alcoa workers were allowed to confront CEO Paul O'Neill at the company's annual meeting. At first defensive about the workers' charges of severe health and safety problems and poor pay, O'Neill later took steps to improve conditions and increase wages by 20 percent.

D. VOTER POWER

In 1997, citizens in several countries expressed their resistance to corporate-driven globalization in the voting booth.

INDIA: In 1997, voters from both fundamentalist movements and progressive people's organizations turned out of office a government that had aggressively pursued pro-globalization policies. Between 1990 and 1995, this government had lowered tariffs from 87 percent to 25 percent and lifted investment barriers, resulting in a flood of foreign capital that undermined Indian-owned enterprises.

FRANCE: Citizens voted in the Socialist Party, which ran on a platform of protecting the French standard of living from low-wage foreign competition by halting privatization, increasing wages and social benefits, and instituting a thirty-five-hour work week.

MEXICO: Opposition parties critical of the ruling party's economic policies gained control of the lower House of Congress and opposition leader Cuauhtemoc Cardenas was elected mayor of Mexico City. As the head of Mexico's largest opposition party during the NAFTA debate, Cardenas was a strong advocate for an alternative approach to globalization, stressing that trade "must be an instrument of development, not an end in itself."

E. CONSUMER POWER

Consumers concerned about the current approach to globalization are increasingly speaking with their pocketbooks, both in terms of what they buy and what they do not buy.

Using Purchasing Power to Influence Companies

SWEATSHOPS In the last few years there has been a groundswell of consumer activism against sweatshops. The extent of public concern was revealed in a landmark survey by Marymount University in 1995. More than three-fourths of those surveyed said they would avoid shopping at stores if they were aware that the stores sold goods made in sweatshops. An overwhelming majority (84 percent) said they would be willing to pay up to an extra $1 on a $20 garment if it were guaranteed to be made in a legitimate shop.[5]

Consumer campaigns against sweatshops have involved a number of tactics, ranging from the use of cards such as the one below, which send a message to retailers, to all-out boycotts.

No Sweatshop! Care Tag

Dear Retailer,

I check the care tag to see how to treat the garments I buy from you. Do you check your manufacturers to see how they treat their workers? Do you enforce a code to assure that manufacturers:

☑ maintain safe working conditions
☑ pay a living wage
☑ respect workers' right to organize

☑ do not use forced or child labor
☑ are independently monitored
☑ report plant conditions to the public

NAME:_____
ADDRESS:_____
_____

Source: Interfaith Center for Corporate Responsibility

Many groups have tried to influence other shoppers by protesting in front of stores. In April 1998, eight New Hampshire residents associated with the American Friends Service Committee were arrested while handing out anti-sweatshop leaflets at a local shopping mall. Although the mall was private property, the group claimed that the right to free speech should protect activities such as peaceful leafleting.

The anti-sweatshop movement is also quite advanced in Europe, where the Clean Clothes Campaign coordinates national coalitions in about a dozen European countries that pressure apparel companies to adopt codes of conduct that are monitored by independent groups.[6]

LABELING Another consumer strategy has been to reward corporations employing "good" business practices by allowing such firms to identify their products with a label. One of the labeling pioneers was the Blue Angel program in Germany, which began in 1977 to encourage consumers to purchase products with a lower negative environmental impact. By 1994, Blue Angel labels could be found on 3,500 products.[7]

Another advanced labeling effort is the Rugmark campaign, which targets child labor in South Asia. The campaign was initiated by the South Asian Coalition on Child Servitude. In the United States, it is coordinated by the Rugmark Foundation, housed at the International Labor Rights Fund. Rugmark-approved rugs have a special label affixed to ensure buyers that adult workers, earning at least the local minimum wage, have knotted this rug. Manufacturers who join Rugmark consent to surprise visits by Rugmark inspecters and local human rights and child advocacy groups. Rugmark also works with U.S. and European importers to provide funding for the education of former child workers in the rug industry.

GREENFREEZE In the early 1990s, the international environmental organization Greenpeace creatively used consumer power to develop a market for ozone-friendly refrigerator technology. Discouraged by the reluctance of existing refrigerator producers to adopt these new technologies, Greenpeace turned to its German members to demonstrate the demand for the environmentally friendly product. When 30,000 members placed advance orders, Greenpeace was able to launch a project to produce new "Greenfreeze" refrigerators in a plant in Eastern Germany. Greenpeace also transferred the technology to developing countries free of charge to help them lessen their dependence on large chemical companies. In response to their success, numerous refrigerator companies now also produce the ozone-friendly models.[8]

GOVERNMENTS AS CONSUMERS: THE BURMA CAMPAIGN
U.S. campaigns against the brutal military regime of Burma have made use of both individual and governmental purchasing power. As of January 1999, twenty-two cities and one state (Massachusetts) had passed "selective purchasing" laws to discourage companies from supporting the military rulers of Burma. These laws, which forbid government contracts with companies conducting business in Burma, are similar to those used to promote divestment from South Africa under Apartheid. Large corporations such as Apple Computers, Eastman Kodak, and Hewlett-Packard all cited the Massachusetts selective-purchasing law as a factor in their divestment from Burma in 1996. Previously, Pepsi-Cola had also pulled out, primarily in response to a boycott led by university students, a key demographic for the soda giant. Pepsi had controlled 80 percent of the Burmese soft drink market. An April 1997 policy directive from the Clinton administration complemented the selective-purchasing laws by banning new U.S. investments in Burma. In November 1998, a court ruled that the Massachusetts statute was illegal because only the federal government has the power to set foreign policy. An appeal is pending. Meanwhile, activist groups such as the Free Burma Coalition are pressuring firms that have refused to terminate their existing investments, such as Unocal, a U.S. firm that is building a billion-dollar natural gas pipeline through Burma to Thailand.

Using Consumer Power to Bypass Global Corporations

Several hundred million dollars worth of trade is now handled outside corporate channels by firms that link small-scale, often worker-owned, producer groups in developing countries directly to consumers. These so-called "alternative trading organizations" eliminate profiteering by distributors, middlemen, and wholesalers and often provide financing, marketing, and other skills training. The goal is to pay producers a stable price, to educate consumers, and to demonstrate that socially and environmentally responsible products can also be profitable. There are now hundreds of such organizations selling products through catalogues and more than 45,000 specialty shops.[9] One of the most successful U.S.-based groups is Massachusetts-based Equal Exchange, which markets coffee from developing country cooperatives to U.S. consumers.

Voluntary Simplicity and Other Moves to Reduce Consumption

Growing numbers of people in the United States and other rich countries are organizing to address the very notion of consumption. In the words of Harvard economist Juliet Schor: "Americans' lives came to be organized, in a very fundamental way, around consumerism.... Millions feel trapped in a cycle of working and spending, running faster and staying in place." Based on these precepts and on an environmental concern over the overconsumption of earth's resources, organizations such as the Center for a New American Dream are helping people readjust their lifestyles as well as change the activities of corporations and governments that promote overconsumption.

Protect Consumers

Increased trade has raised concerns among consumers regarding imports produced in ways that conflict with health and safety standards in the importing country. Food safety has been a major focus of these efforts. For example, European consumers demanded a ban on imports of beef from U.S. and Canadian livestock that had been treated with growth-promoting hormones. In August 1997, the WTO ruled against the European ban, stating that it was discriminatory. However, consumer pressure for such laws continues.

In the United States, consumers are particularly concerned about increased reports of illnesses related to food contamination. Because this has coincided with a surge in food imports that has overwhelmed U.S. customs inspectors, there is a perception that imported food may be more dangerous. A pending bill that would require labels on all fruits and vegetables identifying the country of origin, is gaining support. The effectiveness of such a law in reducing health risks is dubious, because the vast majority of food contamination cases originate in the United States rather than abroad. A likely greater threat is the reduced role of the federal government in food inspection. The government has been transferring some responsibility to corporations to monitor themselves. However, consumer activism on this issue has raised awareness of excessive pesticide use and other hazards, both in the United States and elsewhere. It is also becoming increasingly clear that food produced in unsanitary and unsafe conditions carries hazards both for workers and for consumers.

F. STUDENT POWER

If the 1960s and 1970s were known for student activism against the Vietnam War and the 1980s for divestment from South Africa, the 1990s may be remembered as the decade of student activism against sweatshops and child labor.

Students at fifty U.S. universities have organized demonstrations against the producer of Guess? jeans (a popular brand among college students) with the support of the UNITE garment workers union. The students called for a boycott of Guess? when the U.S. Department of Labor cited the firm's contractors for violating minimum wage and overtime laws, finding that hundreds of thousands of dollars in back wages were owed to their workers. According to UNITE, when immigrant garment workers spoke out about these injustices, Guess? retaliated by shifting its production to Mexico and South America.

On more than eighty campuses, students have been negotiating with their schools to ban the purchase of products bearing the school logo from factories that violate labor rights. At a number of these universities, students have built support for such a ban by staging fashion shows featuring clothes made in sweatshops. As the models parade down the runway, an announcer describes the conditions under which the clothes were made. The first school to adopt such a code was Duke University, which now forbids suppliers from using child labor and requires them to maintain a safe workplace, pay at least minimum wage, recognize the right to form a union, and allow independent monitoring of their plants. Duke students are continuing to press for an expansion of the code to require suppliers to pay a living wage.

One of the most famous student activists on this issue is not even old enough to be in college. Canadian Craig Kielburger founded an anti-child-labor group at age twelve, after reading about a Pakistani boy who had been sold into slavery at age four as a carpet weaver. The boy, Iqbal Masih, escaped from his captors at age ten and began speaking out about child exploitation. He was murdered at age twelve. Kielburger has traveled the world to draw attention to the cause. His work was instrumental in getting a Canadian ban on the sale of fireworks made by children, while his organization, Free the Children, has helped fund a legal aid center in Bangkok and a rehabilitation center in New Delhi for freed child laborers.[10] With Kielburger's help, Free the Children chapters have been founded in twenty-six countries, including the United States.

G. PEOPLE POWER

The fights over globalization have often been battles between political power and money on one side and power in numbers on the other. And nothing has mobilized greater numbers of people than the policies and projects of the World Bank and International Monetary Fund.

PROTESTS AGAINST STRUCTURAL ADJUSTMENT Literally millions of people in the developing world have participated in some form of protest against austerity measures imposed by the World Bank's so-called structural adjustment programs (SAP). In Ecuador, Venezuela, Argentina, Morocco, and Bolivia, citizens outraged by World Bank-imposed cutbacks have paralyzed their national economies through general strikes. In Bolivia, the strike focused on World Bank/IMF's demands for reduced education funding and privatization of the telephone system. The government declared a state of siege to enforce the dictates of the World Bank and IMF, sending troops to beat and tear gas their own people. Nearly 400 labor leaders were arrested and tortured. After international protests and continued solidarity, the government released the leaders and backed down from its plans.[11]

AND AGAINST DAMS Millions have also risen up against World Bank dam projects, including several that would submerge entire villages, forcing residents to resettle, often on undesirable land. In the Philippines, people managed to stop such a project through a long period of active resistance. Villagers barricaded the proposed construction site. Lookouts were assigned to signal others whenever government workers showed up so that everyone in the village could stop what they were doing and help to block construction. During the height of the struggle, women laid down in the road to prevent vehicles from transporting equipment into the site.[12]

© Rini Templeton

CRITIQUE AND DIALOGUE In 1994, the fiftieth anniversary of the World Bank and IMF, citizens groups from all over the world organized a "Fifty Years Is Enough" campaign. In the United States, the campaign has involved more than 200 environmental, development, faith-based, labor and policy organizations. In 1994, the U.S. Congress responded to their demands by restricting funding for the agencies until they improved disclosure, environment, and resettlement policies. An amendment was also approved that requires the United States to use its voting power in the World Bank to promote internationally recognized worker rights. The campaign continues to be a powerful watchdog and critic of these agencies.

In response to escalating criticism, the World Bank has engaged since 1995 in dialogue with citizens organizations to assess the impact of SAPs and involve public participation in future policy making. This citizen participation has been coordinated in the United States by the Development Group on Alternative Policies through the Structural Adjustment Participatory Review International Network, which represents some 2,000 organizations worldwide.

DEBT REDUCTION Another group that has emerged as a voice against the World Bank is Jubilee 2000, a religious coalition demanding cancellation by the year 2000 of all debt owed by the poorest countries. The movement draws its inspiration from the Biblical book of Leviticus (25:8-12), which describes a Year of Jubilee every fifty years. In the Jubilee year, social inequalities are rectified: slaves are freed, land is returned to original owners, and debts are canceled. Jubilee 2000 coalitions exist in dozens of countries.

"Latin America's Foreign Debt: What Can We Do About It?" (comic book produced by the Centro De Estudios Internacionales for Jubilee 2000 in Nicaragua)

Other Forms of Mass Resistance

INDIA Indian citizens have launched some of the most militant and creative campaigns against the World Bank and also against the activities of global corporations. Millions of farmers, fisherfolk, union workers, urban dwellers, and others have engaged in various forms of protest against the growing transnational corporate penetration of the Indian economy. In 1992, Indian activists forced U.S.-based Cargill to drop plans to produce salt in India for export to East Asia. Tens of thousands of protestors re-enacted a famous march led by Gandhi in 1930 aimed at making India self-sufficient in salt and threatened to block the port Cargill planned to use for its exports.[13]

Indian activists also scared away Kentucky Fried Chicken. The city of Bangalore closed KFC's first outlet and canceled its license, claiming that the chain used too much MSG. However, the local government only acted when activists threatened to storm the restaurant to protest the American junk food invasion. Organizers also cited fears that the multinational chain would threaten local food industries and promote factory farming of livestock to cater to KFC's planned sixty outlets in India.[14]

MEXICO: LIBERTY REFERENDUM A creative movement against globalization has also emerged in Mexico. One year after the passage of NAFTA, hundreds of thousands of Mexicans participated in an innovative exercise to express criticism of their country's economic policies. At booths set up outside supermarkets and churches and other community meeting places, citizens cast ballots in a "Liberty Referendum" to endorse a plan for economic recovery and sustainable development. Ratified by a half million Mexican citizens, the alternative plan repudiates the failed "neo-liberal," free market policies pursued by the Mexican government since 1982 and calls for the renegotiation of NAFTA. Although not legally binding, the referendum had a tremendous educational impact that helped strengthen support for the country's political opposition. Two years later, the ruling PRI party lost control of the lower house of Congress. The Liberty Referendum was jointly sponsored by the Mexican Action Network on Free Trade (RMALC) and associations representing small and medium businesses, coffee growers, peasants and bank debtors.

H. LOCAL POWER

Most communities have become convinced that they must compete in the global economy and to do this they must create a favorable business environment to attract multinational, export-oriented firms. At the same time, there is growing resentment toward globe-trotting firms that

- drain resources from local communities to pay off distant executives and stockholders;
- use threats of plant closures to extract government subsidies from local officials and lower wages from workers;
- often leave communities to deal with the consequences of a mass layoff when the company decides it can increase its profits by locating elsewhere.

In dozens of communities around the world, citizens are pursuing a variety of strategies to reduce the vulnerability of their local economies to the whims of global corporations. Michael Shuman provides a comprehensive overview of these efforts, particularly those in the United States, in *Going Local: Creating Self-Reliant Communities in a Global Age*.[15] Here we describe just a few efforts.

Community Ownership

In some communities, workers, citizens groups, or local governments have bought plants to keep them operating when a corporation leaves town. By preventing the ripple effects of a shutdown, communities can benefit even if a plant just breaks even. Some states also allow local governments to use the power of "eminent domain" to take over plants about to be closed, so long as the seizure serves a public purpose and the owners receive "just compensation." Pressured by the United Electrical, Radio, and Machine Workers of America, the City of New Bedford, Massachusetts, threatened to take over a plant owned by Gulf and Western. In response, the company agreed to sell the plant intact to another firm that kept it in operation for seven years. In Boston, community groups used the same power to pressure local officials to take over vacant lots for new affordable housing in the city's most impoverished neighborhood.

Local Currency

Some communities have encouraged residents to support the local economy by creating an alternative paper money system. The most advanced "local currency" program is Ithaca HOURS, based in the small college town of Ithaca, New York. Founder Paul Glover explains, "while dollars make us increasingly dependent on multinational corporations and bankers, HOURS reinforce community trading and expand commerce that is more accountable to our concerns for ecology and social justice." Each HOUR is worth $10, the wage for an

average hour of work. Thus, each bill is good for one hour of labor or its negotiated value in goods and services. Between 1991 and 1997, organizers issued about $55,000 worth of HOURS, and 1,500 people—including 250 business proprietors—used them for an estimated $1.5 million of transactions.

Linking Tax Breaks to Good Jobs

As corporations become ever more mobile, many state and local governments are attempting to pressure firms to keep jobs in their communities by attaching strings to tax incentive deals. Twenty-nine states and eleven cities have begun to include demands on corporations when offering subsidies.[16] These may include requiring the firm to create and maintain a certain number of jobs, pay workers a living wage, and other conditions. Some governments also demand that their money be returned if the company fails to live up to its promises. For example, New York City gave Bank of America a sales tax exemption in 1996 to purchase computers, with the expectation that the investment would help retain jobs in the city. When the bank promptly shipped the computers elsewhere, the city demanded a refund.[17]

I. ARTIST POWER

In 1997, the glamorous crowd at the French equivalent of the Academy Awards got an unexpected lecture on investment liberalization when Brigitte Fossey, a French actress, used her acceptance speech as an opportunity to criticize the MAI as a threat to global cultural diversity.[18] From sequined movie stars to indigenous basket weavers, numerous artists around the world are concerned that the current approach to globalization primarily benefits the U.S. entertainment giants that already dominate world culture. Indeed, it's no surprise that Hollywood's lobbyist, the Motion Picture Association of America, is the most fervent advocate of measures that would:

- lift foreign investment restrictions in cultural industries;
- eliminate controls on imports of cultural products;
- reduce subsidies for local artists.

In nations already overwhelmed by American cultural influences there is the feeling that such measures facilitate homogenization, or Americanization, rather than increased cultural exchange. In both France and Canada, cultural associations were so strongly opposed to such measures in the proposed MAI that the governments of these two nations demanded exemptions for cultural industries. Their stubbornness helped undermine the progress of the MAI talks.

The involvement of artists has greatly enriched the movements around globalization, particularly through their use of the power of creativity to bring information about the global economy to wider audiences.

Superheroes

In Mexico, a superhero named Superbarrio fights against injustice on behalf of the poor. Wearing red tights, a shirt emblazoned with SB, gold wrestling trunks, and a flowing gold cape, Superbarrio is a frequent star of political demonstrations. Under NAFTA, Superbarrio's heroics have taken him on many crusades across the border. Once, he swept into Los Angeles to take water samples for toxic testing in Mexican labs. The local environmental group did not trust the results they were getting from the U.S. government.

In 1994, Superbarrio entered the U.S. presidential race, reasoning that "given that Washington affects us all, north and south, we all should define together who is to live at that famous address." A critique of globalization was at the core of his campaign: "The American Dream cannot be...benefits for transnational corporations and poverty for all the working people of the hemisphere. The American Dream, defined as a universal common right to dignified life, cannot be achieved through the crushing of communities and permitting Wall Street to define what's good for the Americas."

We Are All Superbarrio

Excerpts from Superbarrio's campaign platform:

- Full investigation of financial speculation activities of Wall Street.
- If free trade, then free migration throughout the hemisphere and political integration through free citizenship.
- We are all Americans and as such we will respect the rights of the English-speaking minority in this continent, offering them access to bilingual education. Special education classes will be available to Pat Buchanan, Bob Dole, Newt Gingrich, Bill Clinton, and others like them who have not been able to master another language.

Music

Music can be a powerful weapon. In 1996, a song recorded by a truck driver from Buffalo, New York, helped force a Dutch retailer to the negotiating table over a dispute with U.S. workers. The company, Royal Dutch Ahold, is the largest supermarket chain in the Eastern United States. Residents in the Buffalo area were angered when the firm planned to make changes in its delivery system that would have resulted in significant job loss and threatened local family-owned grocery stores. In response to the dispute, Teamster Kelly Eddington recorded a song in his basement studio to the tune of Harry Belafonte's "Banana Boat Song," except the lyrics went "Ahold Come... and the Jobs Go Away." The song became so popular on Dutch radio that even the Ahold CEO couldn't avoid hearing it. In the end, the Teamsters and a broad coalition of community groups, backed by international support, managed to pressure the company to sign a code of conduct for its U.S. operations.[19]

Ahold Song
words by Kelly Eddington

Ahold, say Ahold
Ahold come and the jobs go away
Come to US with a brand-new plan
Ahold come and the jobs go away
They're going to eliminate the working man
Ahold come and the jobs go away
And they put all the profits in the corporate hands
Ahold come and the jobs go away
Then they'll send the money back to the Netherlands
Ahold come and the jobs go away
(refrain)
One job, two jobs, three jobs four
Ahold come and the jobs go away

They keep disappearing till there are no more
Ahold come and the jobs go away
Soon the mom and pop have to close their little store
Ahold come and the jobs go away
Cuz the unemployed cannot afford to shop no more
(refrain)
Now the unemployed man he has to get welfare
Ahold come and the jobs go away
It's a burden on the taxpayer he must bear
Ahold come and the jobs go away
And the economy gets hurt so it's beyond repair
Ahold come and the jobs go away
So the cross-docking gonna hurt us everywhere
Ahold come and the jobs go away
(refrain)

Some more well-known musicians are also getting into the act. In 1997, the popular rock band Rage Against the Machine used their national tour to send a message to students about sweatshops. The band invited UNITE to appear at each of its sold-out concerts with stickers and leaflets about the Guess? boycott.

Murals

The international solidarity of the U.S.-based UE union and Mexico's Authentic Labor Front (FAT) is expressed visually through murals on the unions' offices in Chicago and Mexico City. American Mike Alewitz was the principal artist on a mural entitled "Trade Unionism Without Borders" at FAT headquarters. The mural depicts workers tearing up borders imposed by bosses and features heroes from both the U.S. and Mexican labor movements. Mexican muralist Daniel Manrique created the mural at the Chicago UE office entitled "Hands in Solidarity—Hands of Freedom."

Comic Books

Cartoonists have lent their artistic skills to support educational efforts on globalization throughout the world. In this booklet by the Coalition for Justice in the Maquiladoras, illustrations of common workplace scenarios help Mexican workers learn about their labor rights so they can more effectively defend themselves against abuses by the primarily U.S.-owned corporations operating on the border.

"What are my rights on the job?"

Theater

Particularly in rural areas and where literacy rates are low, political theater has proved to be an effective way of educating and mobilizing people around globalization issues. For example, Nepali villagers gather around boomboxes in teashops to listen to an audiocassette of a play about hydroelectric power featuring one of Nepal's most famous comedians. Although the World Bank canceled a large-scale dam project (Arun III) in 1995 in response to opposition from Nepali and other nations' nongovernmental organizations, the debate over such projects continues. The play satirizes the World Bank's comedy of errors over Arun III, enabling the audience to laugh at the project's absurdities while raising important questions about the rights of Nepali citizens in determing the country's future development path. The tapes and complementary comic books were produced by a U.S. group, Media for International Development, in conjunction with a Nepali human rights group, INHURED. They have distributed 5,000 tapes and 3,000 comic books throughout the country.

Conclusion:
A Turning Point

For too long, most governments' policies toward the global economy have been held hostage to a rigid free trade and investment formula. The administrations of Reagan, Bush, and Clinton have doggedly pursued such policies at home and abroad, backed by support from the world's largest corporations.

However, as this book goes to press, the debate over the global economy has reached a turning point. In a December 1998 *Wall Street Journal/NBC News* survey, 58 percent of Americans polled indicated that "foreign trade has been bad for the U.S. economy." Polls in other countries are yielding similar results.

Even among the elite stalwarts of trade and investment liberalization, the long-standing free market consensus appears to be unraveling. Except for the rigid IMF and U.S. Treasury Department, two sets of pro-globalization academic and political leaders have broken away. One set remains committed to liberalization of trade flows, but, in light of the global financial crisis, calls for controls on flows of short-term capital. The other set of dissidents argues for the abolition of the IMF, arguing that the agency condones reckless lending by bailing out investors.

For the citizens movement against corporate globalization, the challenge for the future will be to push alternative agendas through this crack in the consensus.

New Alternatives

Many free trade proponents claim that the only alternatives posed by critics are "protectionist" remedies, such as former presidential candidate Pat Buchanan's proposal to build a wall along the U.S.–Mexico border. In fact, the general public is more sophisticated. In a November 1996 poll by BankBoston, only 23 percent of Americans labeled themselves "protectionists," and only 25 percent accepted the label "free traders." More people—45 percent—called themselves "fair traders."

Citizens groups globally are beginning to articulate the principles, policies, and politics of "fair trade." Central to these efforts is the belief that trade and investment should not be ends in themselves but rather tools for promoting ideals such as equality, democracy, good jobs, a clean environment, and healthy communities. The goal is to shift from an emphasis on exports based on the plunder of resources and the exploitation of workers to sustainable economic activity that roots capital locally and nationally. Such an approach rejects the undemocratic fast-track trade authority in the United States, and argues for the development of a democratic and accountable process for negotiating trade and investment agreements in the United States and throughout the world.

Two such initiatives are summarized in appendices to this book. The first is an effort by environmental, labor, farm, and other citizen groups from north and south to propose solutions to the global financial crisis (see Appendix 1). The second arose from a multiyear process between U.S. unions and citizen groups, along with counterparts across the Americas, to create a new framework for trade and investment agreements in the hemisphere (see Appendix 2).

Now is the time for the citizens' backlash to become the "frontlash" for a new global economy. Unions, environmental groups, and other citizens organizations are creating successful coalitions to stop harmful aspects of globalization and to slow down out-of-control flows of capital. They are demanding a place at the negotiating table to craft new rules that steer the benefits of economic activity to the majority, not the minority, and ensure that our planet will be preserved in the twenty-first century.

NOTES

Chapter I

1. Philip Snow, *The Star Raft: China's Encounter with Africa* (New York: Weidenfeld and Nicolson, 1988).

2. See Charles Panati, *Browser's Book of Beginnings: Origins of Everything Under and Including the Sun* (Boston: Houghton Mifflin, 1984); Hans Konig, *Columbus: His Enterprise* (New York: Monthly Review, 1991); Eduardo Galeano, *Open Veins of Latin America* (New York: Monthy Review, 1973); Richard P. Tucker, "Five Hundred Years of Tropical Forest Exploitation," in Suzanne Head and Robert Heizman, eds., *Lessons of the Rain Forest* (San Francisco: Sierra Club, 1990).

3. U.S. Department of Commerce, *U.S. Global Trade Outlook 1995–2000*, (Washington, D.C.: U.S. Department of Commerce, 1995).

4. "Emerging Market" list in *The Economist* (feature in every issue), minus the BEMs and former communist countries.

5. Based on authors' analysis of data in the United Nations Conference on Trade and Development, *Handbook of International Trade and Development Statistics, 1995* (New York and Geneva: United Nations, 1997) pp. 156–159.

6. United Nations Conference on Trade and Development, *Trade and Development Report, 1997*, (New York and Geneva: United Nations, 1997) p. 73. Figure for 1996 calculated by the authors from data in World Bank, *World Development Indicators 1998*, (Washington, DC: World Bank, 1998), pp. 182-198.

7. World Bank, *World Development Indicators 1998*, (Washington, D.C.: World Bank, 1998) pp. 190, 198.

8. Scott Ehlers, "Drug Trafficking and Money Laundering," *Foreign Policy in Focus Brief*, Vol. 3, No. 16, (Institute for Policy Studies and Interhemispheric Resource Center, June 1998).

9. Lumpe, Lora, "Small Arms Trade," *Foreign Policy in Focus Brief*, Vol. 3, No. 10, (Institute for Policy Studies and Interhemispheric Resource Center, May 1998).

10. Jyothi Kanics, "Trafficking in Women," *Foreign Policy in Focus Brief*, Vol. 3, No. 30, (Institute for Policy Studies and Interhemispheric Resource Center, October 1998).

11. Friends of Animals website, "The International Wildlife Trade," http://arrs.envirolink.org/foa/global/global.htm.

12. World Wildlife Fund, "While Supplies Last: The Sale of Tiger and Other Endangered Species Medicines in North America," press release on Web site: www.traffic.org, January 1998.

13. Bruce Rich, *Export Credit and Investment Insurance Agencies: The International Context* (Washington, D.C.: Environmental Defense Fund, March 1998).

14. Miriam Pemberton and Michael Renner, *A Tale of Two Markets: Trade in Arms and Environmental Technologies*, (Washington, D.C.: National Commission for Economic Conversion and Disarmament and Institute for Policy Studies, 1998) p. 71.

15. World Trade Organization, *Trade and Foreign Direct Investment* (Geneva: World Trade Organization, October 1996); and UN, *World Investment Report, 1997*, (New York and Geneva: United Nations, 1997) p. xvi.

16. World Bank, *Global Development Finance* (Washington, D.C.: World Bank, 1997), p. 7.

17. World Bank, *Global Development Finance*, (Washington, D.C.: World Bank, 1998), p. 3.

18. International Confederation of Free Trade Unions, "ICFTU Online," Web site: www.icftu.org, January 21, 1999.

19. Jubilee 2000/USA, Education Packet, 1998.

20. Susan George, *The Debt Boomerang: How Third World Debt Harms Us All* (London: Pluto Press, 1992).

21. Robert J. Samuelson, "Global Capitalism, Once Triumphant, Is in Full Retreat," *International Herald Tribune*, 10 September 1998, p. 8.

22. International Organization on Migration, *Overview of International Migration 1997*, (Geneva: International Organization for Migration, 1997), p. 10.

23. Christopher L. Bach, "U.S. International Transactions, Revised Estimates for 1974–1996," *Survey of Current Business*, U.S. Department of Commerce, (Washington, D.C., July 1997), p. 46.

24. International Organization for Migration, *Overview of International Migration 1997*, (Geneva: International Organization for Migration, 1997), p. 10.

25. *The Ecologist*, Vol. 26, No. 4, (July/August 1996): p 134.

Chapter II

1. Richard C. Longworth, *Global Squeeze: The Coming Crisis for First-World Nations* (Chicago: Contemporary Books, 1998).

2. U.S. Department of Commerce, *Survey of Current Business*, (Washington, D.C., February 1997).

3. Export data: World Bank, *World Development Report 1997*, pp. 242–43.
   Wage data: All except China, from U.S. Department of Labor, Bureau of Labor Statistics "Hourly compensation costs for production workers in manufacturing in U.S. dollars." www.bls.gov. For China: Data for manufacturing workers in the state sector, DOL, BLS, "Foreign Labor Trends: China," FLT 97–8.

Authors calculated hourly wage based on the official forty hour work week, even though a substantial number of workers, particularly in the private sector, work as many as eighty hours per week.

4. BBE Consulting Services.

5. *China Daily Business Weekly*, 3 August 1997, www.chinaeco.com.

6. Martin Khor, *The Economic Crisis in East Asia: Causes, Effect, Lessons*, Third World Network, 1998, p. 2.

7. For more information, see Jerry Mander and Edward Goldsmith, eds., *The Case Against the Global Economy and for a Turn Toward the Local* (San Francisco: Sierra Club Books, 1996).

8. "The Monsanto Files: Can We Survive Genetic Engineering?" *The Ecologist*, Vol. 28, No. 5 (September/October 1998).

Chapter III

1. "Extra! Update," newsletter of Fairness & Accuracy In Reporting, October 1993.

2. "Extra! Update," newsletter of Fairness & Accuracy In Reporting, October 1993.

3. *Extra!*, July/August 1998, p.5.

4. Center for Responsive Politics, *Who Paid for This Election?* 1998, www.crp.org.

5. *New York Times*, 13 April 1992, p. B8.

6. U.S. Bureau of Economic Analysis, *International Accounts Data*, www.bea.doc.gov, 20 May 1998.

7. Robert Scott, Thea Lee, and John Schmitt, *Trading Away Good Jobs: An Examination of Employment and Wages in the U.S., 1979–94*, (Washington, D.C.: Economic Policy Institute, October 1997).

8. Analysis of NAFTA-TAA data done by the authors.

9. Margaret Simms, Joint Center on Political and Economic Studies, quoted in *USA Today*, Feb. 19, 1996.

10. Cited in John Sweeney, *America Needs a Raise* (Boston: Houghton Mifflin, 1996), p. 43.

11. Kate Bronfenbrenner, *Final Report: The Effects of Plant Closing or Threat of Plant Closing on the Rights of Workers to Organize*, Cornell University, New York State School of Industrial and Labor Relations, 30 September 1996.

12. *New York Times*, 1 March 1992.

13. Calculated by the authors from data in the World Bank, *World Development Indicators 1998*, (Washington, D.C.: World Bank, 1998) pp. 188–90.

14. World Bank, *Global Development Finance*, Vol. 1, 1997 (Washington, D.C.: World Bank, 1997), p.7.

15. "Rising Coal Consumption Makes China a World Leader in Pollution," *Washington Post*, 30 November 1997; and Mark Hertsgaard, "Our Real China Problem," *Atlantic Monthly*, November 1997, p. 100.

16. Hertsgaard, "Our Real China Problem," p. 100.

17. Victor Menotti, "Globalization and the Acceleration of Forest Destruction Since Rio," *The Ecologist*, Vol. 28, No. 6, November/December 1998, p. 358.

18. World Resources Institute, *World Resources, 1998–99* (Washington, D.C.: World Resources Institute, 1999), p. 293.

19. John Ross, "Treasure of the Costa Grande," *Sierra Magazine*, July/August 1996, p.22.

20. *Toronto Globe and Mail*, 27 July 1998, p. A1.

21. "OPIC President opens door for new U.S. investment in Colombia," Overseas Private Investment Corporation press release, 15 May 1998.

22. United Nations *World Investment Report 1997*, (New York and Geneva: United Nations, 1997) p. 305 and *Americas Trade*, 6 August 1998, p.20.

23. Luis Lozano, National Autonomous University of Mexico (UNAM), cited in "Mexico Update," a newsletter of Mexico City–based Equipo Pueblo, 7 May 1998.

24. Red Mexicana de Accion Frente Al Libre Comercio, *Myths and Reality: Three Years After NAFTA, Analysis and Proposals from Civil Society*, (Mexico City: RMALC, April 1997), p. 54.

25. *UN Human Development Report* (New York: Oxford University Press, 1995-98) and World Bank, *World Investment Report 1997* (Washington, D.C.: World Bank, 1997), p. 304.

26. Daniel T. Griswold, "The Fast Track to Freer Trade," Cato Institute Briefing Paper No. 34, 30 October, 1997.

27. "A Game of Global Monopoly," *The Economist*, 27 March 1993, p. S17.

28. All data from Steve Beckman, United Auto Workers, Washington, D.C.

29. World Bank, *Global Economic Prospects and the Developing Countries, 1994* (Washington, D.C.: World Bank, 1996) p.5.

30. UN Conference on Trade and Development (UNCTAD), *Trade and Development Report 1997* (Geneva and New York: UN, 1997).

31. Albert Berry, Susan Horton, and Dipak Mazumdar, "Globalization, Adjustment, Inequality, and Poverty," *United Nations Human Development Papers 1997*, (New York: United Nations, 1997) p. 22.

32. United Nations, *Human Development Report 1996* (New York: Oxford University Press, 1996) p. 2.

33. Calculated by authors from data of *Forbes* 5 July 1999 and United Nations, *Human Development Report 1999* (New York: Oxford University Press, 1999).

34. Lawrence Mishel, Jared Bernstein, and John Schmitt, *Finally, Real Wage Gains*, (Washington, D.C.: Economic Policy Institute, 17 July 1998).

35. Laura D'Andrea Tyson (former chair of the Council of Economic Advisers), *Washington Post*, 9 July 1997.

36. United Nations, *Human Development Report 1997*, p. 27; Milanovic, Branko, *Income, Inequality, and Poverty During the Transition from Planned to Market*

Economy, (Washington, D.C.: World Bank, 1998), p. 67.

37. *Business Week*, 19 April 1999, pp. 72, 78.

38. *Fortune*, 12 October 1987, pp. 115–129. *Forbes*, 15 July 1996, pp. 130–186.

39. Citizens for Tax Justice, interview with Director Bob McIntyre, 21 May 1999.

40. Calculated by the authors based on data from *Fortune*, 15 May 1969, pp. 168–172; and *Fortune*, April 27, 1998, p. F-1.

41. Allen R. Myerson, "In Principle, a Case for More 'Sweatshops,'" *New York Times*, 22 June 1997, Section 4, p. 5.

42. All data from Jeff Ballinger, Press for Change (see Directory for more information).

43. Anthony Lewis, "Immigration GOP's Newest Scare Tactic," *Houston Chronicle*, 4 November 1996, p. A22.

44. National Academy of Sciences/National Research Council report, "The New Americans," May 1997.

45. Jeffrey Passel, "Immigrants and Taxes: A Reappraisal of Huddle's 'The Cost of Immigrants,'" (Washington, D.C.: Urban Institute, January 1994), p. 42.

46. Muzaffar Chishti, "Immigration Policy: A Union Viewpoint," Immigration Project, Union of Needletrades, Industrial and Textile Employees (UNITE), memo, 17 November 1997.

47. John Jesitus, "INS Carts Away Hotel Workers in Crude Fashion," *Hotel and Motel Management*, 2 September 1996.

48. U.S. Immigration and Naturalization Service, interview with Russ Bershron, Public Affairs Department, 30 March 1998.

49. Export growth figures from World Bank, *World Development Report 1997* (Washington, D.C.: World Bank, 1997).

50. AFL-CIO, *Trade Deficit Monitor*, Vol. 4, no. 2, April 1998, and Randy Barber and Robert E. Scott, "Jobs on the Wing: Trading Away the Future of the U.S. Aerospace Industry," (Washington, D.C.: Economic Policy Institute, 1995) p. 63.

51. Harley Shaiken, "Going South: Mexican Wages and U.S. Jobs After NAFTA," *The American Prospect*, No. 15, Fall, 1993.

Chapter IV

1. Institute for Local Self-Reliance, "The New Biological Car," *The Carbohydrate Economy* (Summer 1998), p. 4.

2. Paul Sherer, "The Lesson from Chrysler, Citicorp, and Mobil: No Companies Nowadays Are Too Big to Merge," *Wall Street Journal*, 4 January 1999, p. R8.

3. Calculated by the authors from data in *Fortune*, 20 April 1998 and *Forbes*, 27 July 1998 and World Bank, *World Development Report 1998/99* (Washington, D.C.: World Bank, 1999) pp. 212–213.

4. Calculated by the authors from data in *Forbes*, 20 April 1998 and 27 July 1998 and World Bank, *World Development Report 1998/99* (Washington, D.C.: World Bank, 1999) pp. 212–213.

5. James R. Kraus, "World's Top 100 Show Slowest Growth in a Decade," *American Banker*, 6 August 1998.

6. Nationsbank 10-K form 1996.

7. Patrick Bond, "Nationsbank and Community Reinvestment," International Brotherhood of Teamsters, August 1995.

8. Memo from the Congressional Research Service, drawn from data of the Federal Financial Institutions Examination Council "Country Exposure Lending Survey," October 1997.

9. Robert Collier, "Mexico Bailout No Model for Asia," *San Francisco Chronicle*, 8 January 1998, p. 1.

10. Jacques Gelinas, *Freedom from Debt* (London: Zed Books, 1998), p. 46.

11. Congressional testimony of Undersecretary of the U.S. Department of the Treasury Lawrence Summers, 27 March 1995.

12. Development GAP and Friends of the Earth, *On the Wrong Track: A Summary Assessment of IMF Interventions in Selected Countries*, January 1998.

13. David Felix, "IMF Bailouts and Global Financial Flows," *Foreign Policy in Focus Brief*, Vol., 3, No. 5, (Institute for Policy Studies and Interhemispheric Resource Center, April 1998).

14. David Moberg, "Going Bananas," *In These Times*, 21 February 1999.

15. Sam Howe Verhovek, "Pollution Puts People in Peril on the Border with Mexico," *New York Times*, 4 July 1998.

16. *USTR* "Study on the Operation and Effects of the North American Free Trade Agreement," *USTR*, July 1997, p. 91.

17. Joel Millman, "Is the Mexican Model Worth the Pain?" *Wall Street Journal*, 8 March 1999.

18. Gary Hoover, Alta Campbell, and Patrick J. Spain, eds., *Hoover's Handbook of American Business 1994* (Austin, Texas: The Reference Press, 1993) pp. 309, 395 and *Forbes* 500 Top Private Companies, 1997, www.forbes.com.

Chapter V

1. Louis Hartis and Associates for *Business Week*, 3–7 September 1997 and Wirthlin Worldwide for Bank Boston, November 1997.

2. Madeline Drohan, "How the Net Killed the MAI," *Toronto Globe and Mail*, 29 April 1998, p. A1.

3. Andrew Banks and John Russo, "Building Global Trade Union Campaigns and Organizing Structures: Taking the UPS Strike Overseas," in Gregory Mantsios, ed., *A New Labor Movement for the New Century* (New York: Garland, 1998).

4. David Moberg, "Lessons from the Victory at Phillips Van Heusen," *WorkingUSA*, May/June 1998, p. 45.

5. Press release, Marymount University, 17 November 1995.

6. Clean Clothes Campaign, "Request to the Permanent People's Tribunal," Amsterdam, 11 March 1998.

7. United Nations, *Human Development Report 1998*, p. 90.

8. Joshua Karliner, *The Corporate Planet: Ecology and Politics in the Age of Globalization* (San Francisco: Sierra Club Books, 1997), pp. 204–5.

9. United Nations, *Human Development Report 1998*, (New York and Geneva: United Nations, 1998) p. 90.

10. Clint O'Connor, "Teen Activist Makes World Heed His Cause," *Cleveland Plain Dealer*, 15 November. 1997, p. 6E.

11. Alec Dubro, with art by Mike Konopacki, "*The World Bank: A Tale of Power, Plunder and Resistance*," Public Services International, 1995.

12. Leticia Bula-at, "The Struggle of the Kalinga Women Against the Chico Dam Project," *Third World Resurgence*, No. 69, (Malaysia: Third World Network).

13. Karliner, *Corporate Planet*, p. 212.

14. Ong Ju Lynn, "Activists Force India's First KFC Outlet to be Closed Down," Third World Network, *Third World Resurgence*, No. 63, (Malaysia: Third World Network) p. 42.

15. New York: Free Press, 1998.

16. Interview with Greg LeRoy, Good Jobs First, August 1998.

17. Michael M. Phillips, "Localities Force Firms to Keep Promises," *Wall Street Journal*, 26 June 1996, p. A2.

18. "Resnais Film Wins 7 Cesars," *The Gazette* (Montreal), 1 March 1998, p. C8.

19. Andy Banks, "New Voice for Workers, New Vision for Global Unionism," International Brotherhood of Teamsters (no date).

APPENDIX 1

From Speculation to the Real Economy:
AN EMERGING NORTH-SOUTH LABOR-CITIZENS AGENDA ON GLOBAL FINANCE

The following recommendations are drawn from the December 1998 Washington, D.C., conference on "Toward a Progressive International Economy" sponsored by Friends of the Earth, the International Forum on Globalization, and the Third World Network. With input from environmental, labor, farm, and other citizens groups from north and south, they reflect an emerging citizens consensus on what should be done to resolve the global financial crisis.

Principles

The rules and institutions of the financial sector at all levels should:

1. Reorient financial flows from speculation to long-term investment in the real economy at the local and national level
2. Reduce instability and volatility
3. Create maximum space for local and national governments to set exchange rate policies, regulate capital flows, and eliminate speculative activity
4. Keep private losses private
5. Address the imbalance between growing private flows and shrinking public flows

Agenda   International/Multilateral Level

1. Create an International Bankruptcy Mechanism (to reduce "moral hazard") Outside IMF
   —when country cannot repay debts, the mechanism would make sure that in debt restructuring, there is a public and private sharing of costs; the mechanism would prevent a liquidity crisis from becoming a solvency crisis
2. Substantial Debt Reduction Detached from IMF and World Bank Conditions
   —expand debt reduction initiatives substantially to cover a sizable amount of bilateral and multilateral debt, and delink debt reduction from IMF and World Bank conditions
3. IMF Reform
   —enforce Article 6 of IMF charter, namely that the IMF should oversee capital controls, not capital account liberalization (and no expansion of IMF charter on capital flows)
   —if a separate bankruptcy mechanism is created, the IMF can be reduced to a small role of

lender of last resort, overseer of good information, and dispenser of information

—democratize voting, make all information public

4. Tobin Tax (speculation tax; sin tax)

—create an international parliamentary caucus on the Tobin Tax, with a large public campaign (Canadian Parliament voted in March 1999 to take the lead)

Regional

1. Regional Crisis Funds

—support the creation of regional funds outside IMF control when regional crises erupt (the U.S. and IMF opposed the creation of an Asian fund that would have pumped liquidity into Asian crisis nations; the fund could have kept liquidity crisis from turning into solvency crisis)

National

1. Speed Bumps and Capital Controls

—the rules and institutions of the global economy should create maximum space for national government policy making to regulate capital movements; the IMF should help create such space

2. Eliminate Short-term Manipulative Instruments

—after a careful inventory of short-term financial instruments, national governments should set regulations and incentives so as to eliminate those that are meant entirely for speculative purposes (e.g., short selling) that can undermine other economies; the G-22 process may prove helpful in this task

3. Exchange Rate Regimes

—the goal is to reduce the volatility which has characterized exchange rates since the collapse of the Bretton Woods arrangements in the early 1970s

—countries should be given space to determine which regime suits them best

Local

1. Mutual Funds and Pension Funds

—there needs to be massive public education on the possibility of channeling their investments to meet local opportunities and needs

—tax and other incentives can be used to direct mutual and pension fund investments toward productive local activity

—unions in different parts of the world are taking control of pension funds for local investment

APPENDIX 2

Summary: Alternatives for the Americas
BUILDING A PEOPLE'S HEMISPHERIC AGREEMENT

This document reflects an ongoing, collaborative process to establish concrete and viable alternatives, based on the interests of the peoples of our hemisphere, to the Free Trade Area of the Americas (FTAA). This is a working document, designed to stimulate further debate and education on an alternative vision. For a complete copy of the fifty-page document, see www.web.net/comfront or call: 202/898-1566. To submit comments, contact ecoalt@web.net.

GENERAL PRINCIPLES: Trade and investment should not be ends in themselves, but rather the instruments for achieving just and sustainable development. Citizens must have the right to participate in the formulation, implementation, and evaluation of hemispheric social and economic policies. Central goals of these policies should be to promote economic sovereignty, social welfare, and reduced inequality at all levels.

HUMAN RIGHTS: Countries of the Americas should build a common human rights agenda to be included in every hemispheric agreement, along with mechanisms and institutions to ensure full implementation and enforcement. This agenda should promote the broadest definition of human rights, covering civil, political, economic, social, cultural, and environmental rights, gender equity, and rights relating to indigenous peoples and communities.

ENVIRONMENT: Hemispheric agreements should allow governments to channel investment toward environmentally sustainable economic activities, while establishing plans for the gradual "internalization" (taking into account) of the social and environmental costs of unsustainable production and consumption.

LABOR: Hemispheric agreements should include provisions that guarantee the basic rights of working men and women, ensure proper assistance for adjustment as markets are opened up, and promote the improvement of working and living standards of workers and their families.

IMMIGRATION: Economic and financial agreements should include agreements regarding migrant workers. These agreements should recognize the diversity in immigration-related situations in different countries by allowing for variation in immigration policies but also facilitating funding for programs designed to improve employment opportunities in areas that are major net exporters of labor. At the same time, governments should ensure uniform application of their national labor rights for all workers—regardless of immigration status—and severely penalize employers that violate these rights.

ROLE OF THE STATE: Hemispheric agreements should not undermine the ability of the nation-state to meet its citizens' social and economic needs. At the same time, the goal of national economic regulations should not be traditional protectionism, but ensuring that private sector economic activities promote fair and sustainable development. Likewise, agreements should allow nation-states to maintain public sector corporations and procurement policies that support national development goals while fighting government corruption.

INVESTMENT: Hemispheric rules should encourage foreign investment that generates high-quality jobs, sustainable production, and economic stability, while allowing governments to screen out investments that make no net contribution to development, especially speculative capital flows. Citizens groups and all levels of government should have the right to sue investors that violate investment rules.

FINANCE: To promote economic stability, agreements should establish a tax on foreign exchange transactions that would also generate development funds, while allowing governments to institute taxes on speculative profits, require that portfolio investments remain in the country for a specified period, and provide incentives for direct and productive investments. To help level the playing field, low-income nations should be allowed to renegotiate foreign debts to reduce principal owed, lower interest rates, and lengthen repayment terms.

INTELLECTUAL PROPERTY: Agreements should protect the rights and livelihoods of farmers, fishing folk, and communities that act as guardians of biodiversity and not allow corporate interests to undermine these rights. Rules should exclude all life forms from patentability and protect the collective intellectual property of local communities and peoples, especially with regard to medicinal plants. Rules should also ensure that copyright laws protect artists, musicians, and other cultural workers, and not just the publishing and entertainment industries.

SUSTAINABLE ENERGY DEVELOPMENT: A hemispheric agreement should allow members to file complaints against countries that try to achieve commercial advantage at the expense of sustainability. International agencies should cooperate to create regulatory incentives for energy efficiency and renewable energy, and promote related technologies while eliminating policies that subsidize or encourage fossil fuel sales, consumption, and use.

AGRICULTURE: To ensure food security, countries should have the right to protect or exclude staple foods from trade agreements. Hemispheric measures should also support upward harmonization of financial assistance for agriculture (as a percentage of GDP), strengthened protections for agricultural laborers, and traditional rights of indigenous peoples to live off ancestral lands.

MARKET ACCESS: Access for foreign products and investments should be evaluated and defined within the framework of national development plans. Timetables for tariff reduction should be accompanied by programs to ensure that domestic industries become competitive during the transition. Measures are necessary to ensure that non tariff barriers reflect legitimate social interests rather than protections for specific companies.

ENFORCEMENT AND DISPUTE RESOLUTION: If the proposed rules and standards are to be meaningful, they must be accompanied by strong mechanisms for dispute resolution and enforcement that are focused on reducing inequalities and based on fair and democratic processes. Agreements may also include special safeguards for countries suffering as the result of surges in imports.

DIRECTORY OF ORGANIZATIONS

50 Years Is Enough Network

Coalition of U.S. citizens groups to reform the World Bank and International Monetary Fund; linked to groups in 50 countries
1247 E St., SE
Washington, DC 20003
tel: 202/463-2265
fax: 202/544-9359
www.50years.org
wb50years@igc.apc.org

AFL-CIO

Federation of most U.S. labor unions, representing a total of 13.6 million workers
815 16th St. NW
Washington, DC 20006
tel: 202/637-5000
www.aflcio.org

Alliance for Responsible Trade

Broad-based coalition promoting a just and sustainable alternative to free trade and working to strengthen international cooperation among trade activists
927 15th St. NW, 4th Floor
Washington, DC 20005
tel: 202/888-1566
fax: 202/898-1612
www.igc.apc.org/dgap
dgap@igc.org

American Friends Service Committee

Quaker social justice and peace organization; includes programs on economic literacy and U.S.-Mexico border

1501 Cherry St.
Philadelphia, PA 19102
tel: 215/241-7180
fax: 215/241-7177
www.afsc.org
afscinfo@afsc.org

Bank Information Center

Clearing house for information on the policies and projects of the multilateral development banks
733 15th St. NW, Suite 1126
Washington, DC 20005
tel: 202/737-7752
fax: 202/737-1155
bicusa@igc.org

Canadian Center for Policy Alternatives

Produces books and other materials on the MAI, the Canadian alternative federal budget and other issues
804-251 Ouest Laurier Ave.
Ottawa, Ontario K1P 5J6 Canada
tel: 613/563-1341
fax: 613/233-1458
www.policyalternatives.ca
ccpa@policyalternatives.ca

Canadian Labor Congress

Federation representing the majority of Canadian labor unions; publishes "Morning NAFTA," newsletter on economic integration
2841 Riverside Drive
Ottawa, Ontario K1V8X7 Canada
tel: 613/526-7434
fax: 613/521-8949
www.clc-ctc.ca

Center for a New American Dream

National clearinghouse on sustainable consumption
6930 Carroll Ave., Suite 900
Takoma Park, MD 20912
tel: 301/891-ENUF (3683)
fax: 301/891-3684
www.newdream.org
newdream@newdream.org

Center for Democratic Education

*Educates the U.S. public about social and economic
conditions in Central America and the Caribbean and
provides information and training to advocacy groups
in these regions*
8403 Colesville Rd., Suite #720
Silver Spring, MD 20910-3368
tel: 301/589-9383
fax: 301/589-3505
CFEPP@aol.com

Center for International Environmental Law

*Works to advance public participation and
transparency in trade-related institutions*
1367 Connecticut Ave. NW
Washington, DC 20036
tel: 202/785-8700
fax: 202/785-8701
www.igc.apc.org/ciel
cielus@igc.apc.org

Center of Concern

*Catholic research and educational organization
promoting just international finance and trade
systems*
1225 Otis St., NE
Washington, DC 20017

tel: 202/635-2757
fax: 202/832-9494
coc@igc.org

Chilean Alliance for Just and Responsible Trade

*Chilean coalition of environmental, labor, and other
groups on economic integration*
Seminario No. 774
Nuñoa
Santiago, Chile
tel: 562/341-6597
fax: 562/364-1739
www.members.tripod.com/redchile
alianzacj@usa.net

Citizens Trade Campaign

*Coalition of environmental, labor, family farm, consumer,
and religious organizations promoting environmental
and social justice in trade policy*
215 Pennsylvania Ave., SE
Washington, DC 20003
tel: 202/546-4996
fax: 202/547-7392

Clean Clothes Campaign

*Europe-based campaign to promote fair labor practices
in the apparel industry*
PO Box 11584
1001GN Amsterdam, The Netherlands
tel: 3122204122785
fax: 3120 4122786
www.cleanclothes.org
ccc@xs4all.nl

Coalition for Justice in the Maquiladoras

Coalition of religious, environmental, labor, Latino, and women's organizations that pressure U.S.transnational corporations to adopt socially responsible practices within the maquiladora industry
530 Bandera Rd.
San Antonio, TX 78228
tel: 210/732-8957
fax: 210/732-8324
cjm@igc.apc.org

Columban Justice and Peace Office

Works in coalitions on Asian and Latin American human rights, economic, gender, and environmental justice
PO Box 29151
Washington, DC 20017
tel: 202/529-5115
fax: 202/832-5195
www.st.columban.org
columbandc@igc.org

Common Frontiers

Multi-sectoral group engaged in research and action on economic integration in the Americas
15 Gervais Drive, Suite 305
Don Mills, Ontario Canada M3C1Y8
tel: 416/443-9244
fax: 416/441-4073
www.web.net/comfront
comfront@web.net

Co-Op America

Publishes "Boycott Action News," listings of current corporate boycotts
1612 K St., NW, Suite 600
Washington, DC 20006
tel: 800/58-GREEN
fax: 202/331-8166
www.coopamerica.org
info@coopamerica.org

Corporate Watch

Monitors transnational corporations and their social, ecological, and economic impacts
PO Box 29344
San Francisco, CA 94129
tel: 415/561-6567
fax: 415/561-6493
www.corpwatch.org

Council of Canadians

Member organization devoted to advancing alternatives to corporate-style free trade and other issues facing Canada
904-251 Laurier Ave. West
Ottawa, Ontario K1P5J6 Canada
tel: 613/233-2773
fax: 613/233-6776
www.canadians.org
inquiries@canadians.org

Cross-Border Network for Justice and Solidarity

Promotes solidarity between citizens of Kansas City, Missouri and Mexico
PO Box 45753
Kansas City, MO 64171
tel: 816/561-0125
xborder@oz.sunflower.org

Development GAP

Publishes information on structural adjustment and trade liberalization
927 15th St., NW, 4th Floor
Washington, DC 20005
tel: 202/898-1566
fax: 202/898-1612
www.igc.apc.org/dgap
dgap@igc.org

dollars and sense

Bimonthly magazine that explains the working of the U.S. and international economies
One Summer Street
Somerville, MA 02143
tel: 617/628-8411
fax: 617/628-2025
dollars@igc.org

Ecologist

Bimonthly magazine
Unit 18 Chelsea Wharf, 15 Lots Road
London, Sw10 OQJ, United Kingdom
tel: 0171 351-3578
fax: 0171 351-3617
ecologist@gn.apc.org

Economic Policy Institute

Publishes reports and books on international and domestic economic issues
1660 L St. NW, Suite 1200
Washington, DC 20036
tel: 202/775-8810
fax: 202/775-0819
www.epinet.org
epi@epinet.org

Equal Exchange

Worker-owned coop dedicated to fair trade with small-scale coffee farmers in the developing world
250 Revere St.
Canton, MA 02021
tel: 781/830-0303
www.equalexchange.com
eqex@igc.apc.org

Focus on the Global South

Research and advocacy related to international finance and other global issues
Chulalongkorn Univ., Prachuabmoh, Thyathai Rd.
Bangkok, Thailand 10330
tel: 662-218-7363
fax: 662-255-9976
www.focusweb.org

Free Burma Coalition

Coordinates boycotts and other actions to press for democracy in Burma
PO Box 19405
Washington, DC 20036
tel: 202/777-6009
fax: 202/234-5176
www.freeburmacoalition.org
zarni@freeburmacoalition.org

Free the Children

Canadian-based international group to raise awareness of child labor and raise funds to create alternatives
12 E. 48th St.
New York, NY 10017
tel: 800/203-9091
www.freethechildren.org
freechild@clo.com

Friends of the Earth

*International environmental group; includes program
on environmental impact of globalization*
1025 Vermont Ave. NW
Washington, DC 20005
tel: 202/783-7400
fax: 202/783-0444
www.foe.org
foe@foe.org

Global Exchange

*Human rights group dedicated to building
people-to-people ties between First and Third World
nations and promoting sustainable development*
2017 Mission St., Rm. 303
San Francisco, CA 94110
tel: 415/255-7296
fax: 415/255-7498
www.globalexchange.org
info@globalexchange.org

Good Jobs First

*National clearinghouse for organizations
seeking to hold corporations that get tax
subsidies accountable for creating family-wage jobs*
1311 L St. NW
Washington, DC 20005
tel: 202/626-3780
fax: 202/638-3486
www.ctj.org
goodjobs@ctj.org

Highlander Research and Education Center

*Creates educational experiences that empower people
to take democratic leadership toward fundamental
social change*

1959 Highlander Way
New Market, TN 37820
tel: 423/933-3443
fax: 423/933-3424
hrec@igc.org

IBASE

Brazilian institute for socioeconomic analysis
rua Visconde de Ouro Preto #5, 7th Floor
Botafogo, Rio de Janeiro, 22250-180 Brazil
tel: 55 21 553-0676
fax: 55 21 552-8796
atila2ax.apc.org

INFACT

*Led the global boycott against Nestlé for marketing
synthetic infant formula in the developing world; now
working on tobacco corporations*
256 Hanover St.
Boston, MA 02113
tel: 617/742-4583
fax: 617/367-0191
www.infact.org
infact@igc.org

Institute for Agriculture and Trade Policy

*Conducts research, education, training, and coalition-
building in support of environmentally and economically
sustainable agriculture and trade policy*
2105 First Ave. South
Minneapolis, MN 55404
tel: 612/870-0453
fax: 612/870-4846
www.igc.apc.org/iatp
iatp@iatp.org

Institute for Food and Development Policy (FoodFirst)
Think tank and education-for-action center working on hunger and poverty
398 60th St.
Oakland, CA 94618
tel: 510/654-4400
fax: 510/654-4551
www.foodfirst.org
foodfirst@igc.org

Institute for Policy Studies
Independent center for progressive research and education; includes projects on global economy and peace and security
733 15th St. NW, Suite 1020
Washington, DC 20005
tel: 202/234-9382
fax: 202/387-7915
www.ips-dc.org
ipscomm@igc.org

Interconnect
Quarterly newsletter for the support of movement building and resource sharing within the U.S.-Latin American solidarity community
57 S. Main St.
Pittsford, NY 14534
tel: 716/381-5606
fax: 716/381-3134

Interfaith Center on Corporate Responsibility
North American association of religious institutional investors
475 Riverside Drive, Suite 550
New York, NY 10115
tel: 212/870-2295
fax: 212/870-2023
info@iccr.org

Interhemispheric Resource Center
Publishes monthly newsletter on U.S.–Mexico border and other publications on foreign policy
815 Black St.
PO Box 2178
Silver City, NM 88062
tel: 505/388-0208
fax: 505/388-0619
www.zianet.com/irc1
resourcectr@igc.apc.org

International Association of Machinists and Aerospace Workers
Labor union
9000 Machinists Place
Upper Marlboro, MD 20772
tel: 301/967-4500
fax: 301/967-4587
www.iamaw.org

International Brotherhood of Teamsters
Labor union representing 1.4 million U.S. and Canadian workers
25 Louisiana Ave. NW
Washington, DC 20001
tel: 202/624-6800
fax: 202/624-8102
www.teamster.org

International Federation for Alternative Trade

Links producers of handicrafts and food products from the developing world with importers and exporters
30 Murdock Rd.
Bicester, Oxon OX6 7RF, Great Britain
tel: 44-1869-249-819
fax: 44-1869-246-381
www.ifat.org
cwills@ifat.org.uk

International Forum on Globalization

Engages participants from forty countries to carry out public education and research on the global economy
1555 Pacific Ave.
San Francisco, CA 94109
tel: 415/771-3394
fax: 415/771-1121
www.ifg.org
ifg@ifg.org

International Labor Rights Fund

Action and advocacy group focused on strengthening enforcement of international labor rights
733 15th St. NW, Suite 920
Washington, DC 20005
tel: 202/347-4100
fax: 202/347-4885
www.laborrights.org
laborrights@igc.org

International Rivers Network

Works to halt the construction of destructive river development projects and to promote sound river management worldwide
7847 Berkeley Way
Berkeley, CA 94703

tel: 510/848-1155
fax: 510/848-1008
www.irn.org
irn@irn.org

Ithaca Hours

Architects of the local currency system in Ithaca, New York; produces a "Hometown Money Starter Kit" and video
Box 6578
Ithaca, NY 14851
tel: 607/272-4330
www.lightlink.com/ithacahours
hours@lightlink.com

Jubilee 2000

International movement to cancel developing-country debt by the year 2000
222 E. Capitol St. NE
Washington, DC 20003-1036
tel: 202/783-3566
fax: 202/546-4468
www.j2000usa.org
coord@j2000usa.org

Latin America Working Group

Coalition of groups working on U.S. policy towards Latin America
110 Maryland Ave. NE, Box 15
Washington, DC 20002
tel: 202/546-7010
fax: 202/543-7647

Left Business Observer

Monthly newsletter on domestic and international economics and politics.
250 W. 85th St.
New York, NY 10024
tel: 212/874-4020
fax: 603/506-6212
www.panix.com/~dhenwood/LBO_home.html
dhenwood@panix.com

Maquiladora Health and Safety Support Network

A volunteer network of 400 occupational health and safety professionals who provide information, technical assistance, and on-site instruction regarding workplace hazards in the maquiladoras.
PO Box 124
Berkeley, CA 94701-0124
tel: 510/558-1014
http://members.aol.com/ishmaelmd/INDEX.HTM

Maryknoll Justice and Peace Office

Works to bring the voice of Maryknoll missionaries and the people they serve to decision-making tables in the U.S. and other governments, the UN, and international financial institutions
PO Box 29132
Washington, DC 20017
tel: 202/832-1780
fax: 202/832-5195
www.maryknoll.org

Mexican Action Network on Free Trade

Coalition of labor, environmental, and human rights groups promoting an alternative to free trade
Esplanada 705
MEXICO 11000, D.F.

tel: 525-355-1177
fax: 525-355-1177
rmalc@laneta.apc.org

Multinational Monitor

Monthly magazine that features exposés of global corporations
PO Box 19405
Washington, DC 20036
tel: 202/387-8030
fax: 202/234-5176
www.essential.org

National Labor Committee

Uses popular campaigns to promote labor rights and pressure companies to adhere to international standards
275 7th Ave.
New York, NY 10001
tel: 212/242-3002
fax: 212/242-3821
www.nlcnet.org
tnlc@erols.com

National Network for Immigrant and Refugee Rights

Coordinates national activity on workplace raids and migrant rights
310 8th St., Suite 307
Oakland, CA 94607
tel: 510/465-1984
fax: 510/465-1885
www.nnirr.org
nnirr@igc.org

Northwest Environment Watch

Regional environmental research center focusing on global consequences of North American consumerism

1402 3rd Ave. #1127
Seattle, WA 98101
tel: 206/447-1880
fax: 206/447-2270
www.northwestwatch.org
new@northwestwatch.org

Polaris Institute

Research and advocacy aimed at countering corporate rule

4 Jeffrey Ave.
Ottawa, Ontario K1K0E2, Canada
tel: 613/746-8374
fax: 613/746-8914
tclarke@web.net

Preamble Center for Public Policy

Research and education group focusing on domestic and international economic issues, including the MAI and IMF

1737 21st St., NW
Washington, DC 20009
tel: 202/265-3263
fax: 202/265-3647
www.rtk.net/preamble
preamble@rtk.net

Press for Change

Conducts research and advocacy related to labor conditions in Asia

PO Box 161
Alpine, NJ 07620
tel: 201/768-0715
fax: 201/768-5812
www.nikeworkers.org
jeffreyd@mindspring.com

Program on Corporations, Law and Democracy

Produces publications and conducts workshops that challenge the excessive power of corporations

PO Box 246
S. Yarmouth, MA 02664-0246
tel: 508/398-1145
fax: 508/398-1552
people@poclad.org

Project South

Community-based popular education and action group focusing on social justice in the U.S. South

9 Gammon Ave. SW
Atlanta, GA 30315
tel: 404/622-0602
fax: 404/622-7992
www.peacenet.org/projectsouth
projectsouth@igc.apc.org

Project Underground

Exposes corporate human rights and environmental abuses in the mining and oil industries

1847 Berkeley Way
Berkeley, CA 94703
www.moles.org/ProjectUnderground
project_underground@moles.org

Public Citizen/Global Trade Watch

Education and lobbying group fighting for better international trade and investment policies

215 Pennsylvania Ave. SE
Washington, DC 20001
tel: 202/546-4996
fax: 202/547-7392
www.citizen.org
gtwinfo@citizen.org

RENACE

Chilean network of environmental groups

Seminario 774, Nuñoa

Santiago, Chile

tel: 562 223-4483

fax: 562 225-8909

renace@rdc.cl

Resource Center of the Americas

Educational group focusing on W. Hemisphere; publishes bimonthly newsletter on labor solidarity in the Americas

317 17th Ave. SE

Minneapolis, MN 55414-2077

tel: 612/627-9445

fax: 612/627-9450

www.americas.org/arcta/

Sierra Club

National environmental group, includes programs on trade

85 2nd St., 2nd Floor

San Francisco, CA 94105

tel: 415/977-5500

fax: 415/977-5799

www.sierraclub.org

information@sierraclub.org

Southwest Network for Environmental and Economic Justice

Network of community-based groups in the Southwestern United States; includes project on the U.S.–Mexico border

PO Box 7399

Albuquerque, NM 87194

tel: 505/242-0416

fax: 505/242-5609

Support Committee for Maquiladora Workers

Coordinates solidarity work on labor struggles in Tijuana, Mexico

3909 Centre St., #210

San Diego, CA 92103

tel: 619/542-0826

fax: 619/295-5879

Tennessee Industrial Renewal Network

Community-labor coalition that works on economic justice issues in Tennessee

1515 E. Magnolia Ave. Suite 403

Knoxville, TN 37917

tel: 423/637-1576

fax: 423/522-74476

tirn@igc.org

Third World Network

Network of developing-country nongovernmental organizations; publishes Third World Resurgence, *monthly magazine that articulates a Southern perspective on environment, politics, and current affairs*

228 Macalister Rd.

10400 Penang, Malaysia

tel: 60-4-2266728

fax: 60-4-2264505

www.twnside.org

twn@igc.apc.org

Transnational Institute

International network of scholar-activists working on developing viable solutions to global problems

20 Paulus Potterstraat

1071DA Amsterdam, Netherlands

tel: 3120 6626608

fax: 3120 6757176

www.tni.org

tni@worldcom.nl

US/Guatemala Labor Education Project

*Carries out corporate campaigns and network building
in support of Guatemala labor struggles*

PO Box 268-290

Chicago, IL 60626

tel: 773/262-6502

fax: 773/262-6602

usglep@igc.org

UNITE

Union representing textile and apparel workers

888 16th St. NW, Suite 303

Washington, DC 20006

tel: 202/347-7417

fax: 202/347-0708

www.uniteunion.org

unite@bellatlantic.net

United Auto Workers

Union representing U.S. auto workers

8000 E. Jefferson

Detroit, MI 48214

tel: 313/926-5000

www.uaw.org

uaw@uaw.org

**United Electrical, Radio and Machine
Workers of America**

U.S. union involved in Mexico solidarity work

One Gateway Center, Suite 1400

Pittsburgh, PA 15222-1416

tel: 412/471-8919

fax: 412/471-8999

www. ranknfile-ue.org

ueintl@igc.apc.org

United for a Fair Economy

*Popular education and research group working to
reduce inequality*

37 Temple Pl., 5th Floor

Boston, MA 02111

tel: 617/423-2148

fax: 617/423-0191

www.stw.org

stw@stw.org

United Steelworkers of America

*Labor union representing 700,000 U.S. and
Canadian workers*

5 Gateway Center

Pittsburgh, PA 15222

tel: 412/562-2400

fax: 412/562-2598

www.uswa.org

Witness for Peace

*Organizes delegations to Central America and the
Caribbean and other educational activities on globalization*

110 Maryland Ave. NE, #304

Washington, DC 20002

tel: 202/544-0781

fax: 202/544-1187

w4peace.org/wfp

witness@w4peace.org

World Federalist Association

Dedicated to strengthening the United Nations

418 7th St. SE

Washington, DC 20003

tel: 202/546-3950

fax: 202/546-3749

www.wfa.org

wfa@wfa.org

ACKNOWLEDGMENTS

This book has derived great benefit from the countless people who have
attended workshops and seminars that we have led on this subject
over the last decade. We also thank colleagues at the Institute
for Policy Studies, particularly Richard J. Barnet and Saul Landau, who
have sharpened our thinking with good questions and ready feedback.
IPS interns Tammy Lyn Donohue, Phoebe Haupt, Dori Kornfeld,
and Farah Nazarali did invaluable research for the book. American
University professor Robin Broad helped to shape the analysis
of several of the sections. And insightful comments were provided
by Steve Beckman, United Auto Workers; David Ranney, University
of Illinois, Chicago; Njoki Noroge Njehu, 50 Years Is Enough Network;
and Jeff Ballinger, Press for Change.